BACKROADS & BYWAYS OF

Missouri

BACKROADS & BYWAYS OF

Missouri

Drives, Day Trips & Weekend Excursions

Scenic Vistas

Historic Sites

Country Inns

Down-Home Restaurants

Selective Shopping

Archie Satterfield

The Countryman Press
Woodstock, Vermont

We welcome your comments and suggestions.
Please contact Editor
The Countryman Press
P.O. Box 748, Woodstock
VT 05091, or e-mail
countrymanpress@wwnorton.com

ISBN 978-0-88150-775-1

Book design, map, and composition by Hespenheide Design
Cover photo © 2008 by William Howse/Image Finders
Interior photos by the author unless otherwise specified

Published by The Countryman Press, P.O. Box 748, Woodstock, VT 05091

Distributed by W. W. Norton & Company, Inc., 500 Fifth Avenue, New York, NY 10110

Printed in the United States of America

10 9 8 7 6 5 4 3 2

This book is for Wilma Robbins Hooper, who permitted me to attend the one-room schoolhouse at Howards Ridge in Ozark County a year early. She began teaching all eight grades in the tiny building at the age of 17 and continued for more than 50 years. She later taught only first grade because she wanted to enhance children's educational experiences through her combination of teaching skills and her deep love for all children.

Map of Missouri

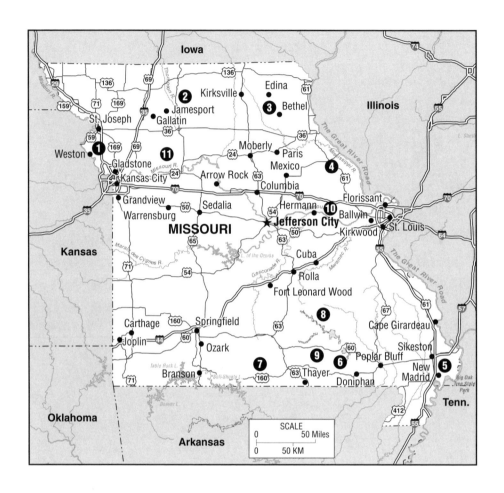

Contents

Introduction

History is the engine that drives Missouri's tourism. The state is almost in the exact center of the nation and has a very rich history. It has been a gathering place for pioneering settlers and a launching pad for the westering urge that afflicted the nation, indeed much of the world, during the 19th century. Before that, the trappers used the Mississippi and Missouri Rivers as highways, and they left their imprint on the state: the French in St. Louis and towns along the Mississippi, the Germans who settled in the interior of the state, and the British who wandered almost due west after settling the East Coast. Of the Native Americans who lived in the area, the proud, tall, obsessively clean Osage made the most lasting impression on the people who eventually, inevitably, drove them out of their homeland.

Nearly all of the highways and byways discussed in this book lead to places that commemorate things that happened before the turn of the 20th century. History never stops, of course, but we tend to think in terms of things that happened during the pioneering era as history. Anything that's happened since is just old news (or something like that).

This book has been written with the assumption that it will be taken along on car trips, and that one person will read place descriptions and historical sketches aloud to the driver and whomever else happens to be along for the ride. This is a very satisfying way to travel and brings the countryside and towns to life.

The book was also written with the attitude that getting there should be at least half the fun, and that there isn't much fun in driving fast on main highways. Thus, the roads had to be interesting themselves, and they had to be slow. It is for this reason that some major destinations aren't mentioned: Highways leading to them are too big and too fast to be interesting, and once you're there you must compete with many other tourists.

The trips in this book are laid out in a generally clockwise manner. The first trip is out of Kansas City, followed by a drive across the top of the state, then down along the Mississippi River. From the Mississippi River valley, we follow a road from the swamps of that region to the middle of the Ozark Mountains in the Branson area. Several roads leading off this east–west route head back to St. Louis and that general area. Finally, the book ends with a journey down along the Missouri River from the middle of the state to Kansas City.

Missouri is a beautiful state in all seasons of the year. Spring and autumn are particularly beautiful in the Ozarks; indeed, some argue that since Missouri has a wider variety of plant life than New England, its autumn is more spectacular. Winter can be excruciatingly cold, especially along the Missouri and Mississippi Rivers, with the wet wind coming off these big rivers as penetrating as armor-piercing weaponry. Conversely, August and September can be smotheringly hot, for the same reason winter is felt deep in your bones—all that humidity. If you are traveling in Missouri in these months, you will bless the people who developed assorted air-cooling devices for automobiles.

Most of Missouri is still rural in character, so you should be prepared for a driving quirk that is very rural in nature. When Missourians prepare to turn off the highway, they slow almost to a complete stop before turning. They drive as though they have a dozen eggs rolling around in the seat beside them, and sometimes that may be the case. Be careful that you don't rear-end the car ahead of you before you become accustomed to the way the drivers here turn: they flick on the turn signal, slow to a crawl, and slowly, ever so slowly, make the turn and then resume speed.

Another word of caution: While following a vehicle, any vehicle, including motorcycles, you should assume that the driver ahead is accustomed to towing trailers—semis, horse trailers, or the garden variety. Often they will swing wide to the left, even edging into the oncoming lane, when they prepare to make a right turn. Force of habit. Even motorcycle riders do it. True, not all people in rural areas drive this way, but you will find enough of them to keep up your guard.

Missouri highways seem to have been built with lollygaggers in mind, because there is always something worth looking at: the landscape itself, guessing what each crop is; that beautiful carpenter-Gothic farmhouse and wondering why it stands empty; that country road, deciding if you should take a chance and drive down it for no reason other than curiosity, and so forth. It is good advice to remember, while going on a car trip in Missouri, that the best way to travel is in the manner of small boys and most happy dogs: stop here for a while, turn around, and go back for a second look at something; zigzag for no particular reason; stop and stare at cattle, or go back for something you thought you saw in a ditch. The best travelers are lollygaggers. Since history is what Missouri has in abundance, and sells constantly, each chapter gives historical perspective on the area being traveled, but also a sense of what the place looks like and how it functions today rather than only yesterday.

A note on listings for lodging, dining, and shopping: Since the routes taken are largely rural, the lists of these places are often sparse or nonexistent, for the simple reason that some towns visited are too small or too far off the beaten path to have many amenities for visitors. In these cases, you are advised to plan your trip so that you can arrive in larger towns toward evening. Sometimes you will find while traveling that you are not in the mood to stay in a cozy bed-and-breakfast or an elaborate inn; all you want is to be alone in a room with a lock on the door and clean sheets. Other times you will wish for a privately owned establishment operated by friendly and helpful people, and on these occasions you will look forward to interacting with the host and other guests. Usually you will find both options on these routes. In keeping with the title of the book, larger cities are generally ignored, so big-city hotels and restaurants are not listed.

Finally, credit must be given to the book *Roads & Their Builders*, published by the Missouri State Highway Commission's Division of Public Information, if for no other reason than the pleasure in reading this statement made by Isaac van Bibber, Jr., while he was trying to promote travel along the Boonslick Road in about 1865:

Who will join in the march to the Rocky Mountains with me? A sort of high-pressure, double-cylinder, go-it-ahead, forty-wild-cats-tearin' sort of feller? Wake up, ye sleepy heads. . . . Git out of this brick kiln . . . these mortality turners and murder mills, where they render all the lard out of a feller until he is too lean to sweat. Git out of this warming-pan, ye hollyhocks, and go out to the West where you may be seen.

Now *that's* enthusiasm for the open road.

Kansas City, Weston, and St. Joseph

Estimated length: 55 miles
Estimated time: half day

Getting there: From Kansas City, take US 71 north to Exit 5, and then turn west on MO 45 and follow it along the Missouri River to Weston, Lewis and Clark State Park, and several other small towns, and end the trip in St. Joseph.

Highlights: Missouri River bottomlands, picturesque small towns, the historic town of **Weston**, Lewis and Clark State Park, and historic **St. Joseph**.

The area this chapter covers was part of the Platte Purchase, which was made in 1836 when land promoters and advocates of the Manifest Destiny doctrine wanted to keep extending the boundaries of states and the entire nation westward. At that time, the border of Missouri did not follow the Missouri River all the way to the top of the state. Instead, the border ran due north from where the Missouri River takes a sharp turn northward, leaving some 3,000 square miles, or 2 million acres, between the border and the river.

Patee House Museum covers an entire block in St. Joseph.

Governor William Clark, of the Lewis and Clark Expedition, arranged the purchase of the Platte land and paid the tribes $7,500 for the land; in March 1837, President Martin Van Buren signed the paperwork and proclaimed the land part of Missouri.

The first surprise for many people seeing the **Missouri River** for the first time is its size. Since it is one of the most famous rivers in America and was the trappers' and traders' route west, in the minds of most people it is always a large, broad river. Remember the famous words, "across the wide Missouri," from the song "Shenandoah"? Although it might be difficult for most of us to throw a rock across it, the river is still much smaller in actual size, given its larger-than-life reputation as a wet highway across the American West.

That minor quibble aside, this is a beautiful drive, one that should be made slowly so that the landscape and beautiful farms with miles and miles of white fences can be savored, rather than half-imagined while tailgating along in heavy traffic. Much of this route is through hilly country. The highway runs along the inland edge of the river bottomland rather than cutting across the middle, where it would waste good farmland and be subject to flooding. Because of the hills and the lack of earth-moving equipment when it was built, much of the road is of a double-yellow-line nature. If you are behind a slow driver or a tractor en route to another field, plan on taking your time.

Although much of the bottomland is still farmed, many homes built on the low hillsides look suburban, and one can speculate that they are owned by people who work in Kansas City and commute daily. A favorite pastime of residents here appears to be painting fences, because this part of Missouri has mile upon mile of white wooden fences; these sometimes give the landscape the look of an artist's painting, and not just painted fences. Most of the hills are thick with oak, which have an almost fluffy look in the haze of the humidity and assorted air pollutants that so often blanket Missouri. In October the hills become a patchwork quilt of different colors in the dense woods. Here, as in the Ozarks, the woods are too thick to walk through without tearing your clothes. Although dictionaries offer other origins of the word *thicket*, once you have gone for a walk in woods like these, complete with old blackberry vines, sumac, poison ivy or oak, assorted sprouts of new trees, and maybe even wild strawberries whose vines will trip you, there will be no doubt in your mind that "thicket" was a word invented in Missouri, whether it actually was or not.

Some very small towns are scattered along the river; one of the prettiest is **Parley**, with a population of 217. Parley is a sensible town because it was built on a hill high enough to escape the floods, which makes the town, with its distinctive brick church, more picturesque than if it had been built down on the flats. It is easy to imagine the conversations held by founders of the town who would not have wanted to waste an acre of that rich river bottomland by covering it with something as unnecessary as a house.

The high point of this trip is **Weston**, roughly halfway between Kansas City and St. Joseph on MO 45. Weston was platted in 1837 on a series of steep hills overlooking the Missouri River and was settled by slave-holding southerners, followed by a scattering of Germans, Austrians, and Swiss. It soon became one of Missouri's most important river towns because of its location just above where the Missouri takes a right turn to the north. For a while, Weston was the second largest port in the state, behind St. Louis.

The first farmers in the area raised tobacco and hemp. Weston is the only place in Missouri that still grows tobacco, some 2 million pounds annually, and probably the only place west of the Mississippi

Benner House B&B in Weston

to still raise the plant; in the fall you'll see bunches of the big leaves hanging in barns to dry. During its pioneering heyday, steamboats landed regularly at Weston, and the town had a brewery and two flourmills.

The **McCormick Distillery**, still in operation, was founded in 1856 by the entrepreneur Ben Holliday. He also dabbled in the Pony Express and founded the stagecoach company that bore his name before he graduated to railroads. It was in railroads that Holliday gained the most fame, but it was also his undoing because he lost everything in the stock market crash of 1873. Holliday managed to keep the McCormick Distillery, which was managed by his brother Donald.

By the time the Civil War broke out, Weston had a population of around 5,000 and was an important stop on the Oregon Trail. Almost as many wagon trains heading west crossed the Missouri at Weston as up north at St. Joseph.

Then the town was hit by a series of disasters. A cholera epidemic struck and killed hundreds. Most of the downtown area was destroyed in two major fires early in its history. These catastrophes were followed by five floods. When the last flood subsided, the river channel had moved about 2 miles away to the site of a previous channel, where it has stayed ever since.

The Civil War split many families. The population of Weston dwindled to around 1,000 by 1890 and stayed there for 90 years, until 1892, when the Weston Development Company was formed to breathe new life into the town. An inventory of the town's advantages included more than 100 residences dating before the Civil War and the largest number of antebellum homes in Missouri. The Weston Development Company worked with community organizations to designate the downtown area a historic district and to place it on the National Register of Historic Places.

Weston has antique and collectible shops galore, art galleries, a number of bed-and-breakfast inns (B&Bs), a recently restored hotel, the McCormick Distillery, **Mission Creek** and **Pritle's wineries**, an orchard with a retail outlet, three museums, restaurants and cafés, gift shops along Main Street, and special events throughout the year. You can also buy locally produced spirits where they are produced. All of this means that it is the major destination town north of Kansas City. Several of the attractions are listed at the end of this chapter.

Five miles north of Weston on MO 45, you'll find a group of hills being used for something other than building homes with views and raising oak timber. The **Snow Creek Ski Area** is one of the few ski areas in Missouri. It has a 300-foot vertical drop, two triple chairlifts, one double chairlift, nine intermediate trails, and three rope tows. The ski lodge has a bar and lounge and cafeteria, plus a rental shop, first-aid room, and ski school. It is open for night skiing and has snow-making equipment.

MO 45 heading north straightens out after leaving Weston, and by the time it reaches **Lewis and Clark State Park** and joins US 59, the sense of being on a country road begins to dissipate. The park, created in 1934, covers 190 acres surrounding Sugar Lake and has camping, boating, fishing, and swimming. Fishermen try to hook carp, buffalo, and channel catfish from the lake, while other visitors enjoy the sandy beaches, bird watching, and picnicking. Groups may reserve the shelter that was built by the Civilian Conservation Corps during the Great Depression of the 1930s.

This is one of hundreds of places along the Missouri honoring the explorers Meriwether Lewis and William Clark: It is doubtful that any of the pioneers of the West had more places named in their honor than these two dedicated men.

Just after the United States acquired the French territories of the Louisiana Purchase in 1803, President Thomas Jefferson appointed Captain Lewis to lead an expedition to the Pacific Ocean and bring back volumes of reports, so that the government would know whether to try and obtain the remaining land between the two oceans. Nobody really knew what was out there in the vast wilderness between the Mississippi and the Pacific, and the search for the Northwest Passage from the East Coast to the West Coast was still very much a subject of speculation. Explorers knew of the mighty Columbia River, but they did not know what lay between it and the Missouri. Jefferson wondered if the Missouri might complete the route between the oceans. He hoped that it was simply a matter of crossing a low divide between the two river systems.

This concern with controlling the whole continent was part of the Manifest Destiny doctrine making the rounds in America, a justification for taking land that didn't belong to the U.S. In staking a claim across the whole continent, the U.S. had to deal not only with the French (who sold their claimed land to President Jefferson in the Louisiana Purchase deal) but also with the Spanish, who had claims on the Southwestern desert and the California coast; in addition, there were the English, who then had most of Canada and were elbowing their way down the coast to meet the Spanish, and the Russians, who had Alaska and were in and out of the Hawaiian Islands, without making an actual claim, and along the Pacific coast down to California.

The Lewis and Clark Expedition was clearly a major undertaking. Although an army officer was leading it, Captain Lewis, Jefferson did not want it to be a military venture. It was to be an exploration only: go in as quietly as possible, meet with local governments and tell them about the change in ownership, see what was there, and come home with complete reports on virtually everything—zoology, botany, geography, cartography, celestial movements, anthropology, ethnography, politics, and so on.

Jefferson let Lewis select his own crew; Lewis immediately chose as his co-commander an old friend, Lieutenant Clark. Lewis told Clark that nobody should know that their ranks weren't equal, and that they would both be known as captains. Lewis began his trip in Washington, D.C., and then went up to Pittsburgh to start assembling his crew and to buy a keelboat. They floated it down the Ohio River to the Mississippi, with an occasional stop to take on more men, and once even stopped to look at dinosaur bones. When the boat entered the Mississippi, the crew had to paddle and tow the boat upriver to a camp in the St. Louis vicinity. The captains decided to put themselves some distance from the temptations of St. Louis and set up winter camp on the Wood River across the Mississippi. They spent the winter of 1803–04 trying to turn a group of independent woodsmen, trappers, and farmers into a disciplined unit.

In addition to the experienced woodsmen they hired, Lewis and Clark also took on a military detachment to escort the party up the Missouri River to their winter quarters and help them with the enormous amount of food, clothing, and scientific equipment they had to carry.

During that summer of 1804, they rowed and towed their boats upstream and made note of many places still recognizable today: caves they camped in, streams entering the Missouri, and prominent landmarks. They were into the Dakotas by fall, where they built a small fortress, named it Fort Mandan in honor of the local tribe, and wintered over.

When spring arrived, the extra men floated back down the Missouri to St. Louis, leaving Lewis and Clark and their party of 28 men, one woman (named Sacajawea), and one child (Sacajawea gave birth to a son that winter). The explorers struck out into the unknown when ice cleared from the Missouri. They spent the spring, summer, and fall of 1805 going up the Missouri almost to its headwaters, bought horses from Sacajawea's relatives, and then crossed a low pass into what is now Idaho. They almost starved to death in the Bitterroot Range before staggering into the Nez Perce villages along the Clearwater River. They ate fish that probably didn't agree with their weakened bodies, and many fell ill. When they had purchased or built enough canoes, they launched them into the Snake River, with some men still too weak to do anything other than lie in the canoes and hope for the best. They survived the terrible rapids of the Snake, entered the Columbia, and got safely around and through the rapids and waterfalls of the Columbia Gorge. They arrived at the mouth of the Columbia River in November 1805.

Lewis and Clark spent the winter of 1805–06 at Fort Clatsop, which they built near present-day Astoria, Oregon, and left for home in the spring of 1806. They paddled up the Columbia and the Snake Rivers and retraced their path back into Montana. There, they split into two parties: Clark's group went south to catch the Yellowstone River and followed it down to its confluence with the Missouri, near what is now the Montana–North Dakota state line. Lewis led the group going north into the Blackfoot country on the Marias and Milk Rivers. They got into a running fight with a Blackfoot band, and the group almost rode their horses to death on the dash back to the Missouri. They made the rest of the downriver trip with Captain Lewis lying prone on the floor of a raft, a musket ball in his buttocks. It was put there by a crewman named Pierre Cruzatte, who was blind in one eye and weak-sighted in the other. Cruzatte had mistaken the buckskin-clad Lewis for a deer.

The two captains have been heroes to American people for two centuries, if for no other reason than that they got their orders from President Jefferson—among the most detailed orders in American history —and they followed the orders exactly. When you study the history of the expedition and realize how difficult the trip was, you have no choice but to be impressed with the dedication of these men. They worked very hard for more than two years under extreme conditions, and never once complained that too much was expected of them or that they had a stomachache, or that they simply weren't in the mood to write in their journals that day.

The explorers treated the Native Americans with courtesy, but the tribes must have been a little curious about these men who told them they now had a Great White Father when they didn't even know one had existed. But, to the explorers' credit, they never treated them as childlike savages or cannon fodder. They were under orders from Jefferson not to get involved in battles with the natives. They did so only once, when a band of Blackfoot tried to ambush them.

This doesn't mean that Lewis and Clark were doormats for the Native Americans. To the contrary: For example, on the explorers' return trip up the Columbia and Snake Rivers, a native ridiculed them for eating dog meat (the natives' diet of fish and camas roots was giving the explorers the "back door trots"). Clark almost came to blows with the man who ridiculed him, and flung a live puppy at him. Message delivered, message received. The native backed off.

Clark was probably a bit easier to take than the serious, perhaps unstable Lewis, who tended to be a prude. Clark seemed to enjoy the personalities of his companions and the Native Americans they met along the way, accepting them as they were. Clark had a sense of humor, which showed from time to time in the journals, and which he couldn't always contain. When describing the social skills of the Clatsop tribe, which were sorely lacking by Washington, D.C. standards, Clark gleefully described their gastronomical and bathroom habits.

Along the explorers' route from Wood River, near Alton, Illinois, to Astoria, Oregon, you'll see special highway markers commemorating their trip. Most of their campsites have been identified—all along the Missouri River to its headwaters in Montana and the Clearwater, Snake, and Columbia Rivers—as well as sites of side trips they took in Montana.

How well did they do their work? According to the great Lewis and Clark scholar Paul Russell Cutright, they accomplished these things: They initiated the first official relations between the U.S. government and Native Americans along the route from Missouri to the Columbia watershed; they discovered the Shoshoni, Flathead, Nez Perce, Yakima, Walula, and Wishram tribes; and they undertook first language studies in at least six new linguistic groups.

In addition, they ended the long search for the fabled Northwest Passage. They established that the North American continent was much wider than previously believed—many thought it ended just beyond the Rocky Mountains—with the discovery that two mountain systems separated the Missouri headwaters from the Pacific. They discovered and thoroughly described at least 170 plants new to botanists and at least 120 new birds and animals.

As a footnote to history, because Lewis started at Washington, D.C., this trip made him the first American on record to travel overland from the Atlantic to the Pacific.

After you pass Lewis and Clark State Park, the remaining 20 miles into **St. Joseph** aren't particularly interesting because you will be driving alongside a railroad track on a flat, straight highway, which suddenly becomes quite busy. You will cross a bridge over Contrary Creek, and drive between black-dirt farms some distance inland from the Missouri River. With little advance warning—no suburbs or other signals that a city is coming—the highway takes you into the center of St. Joseph, one of Missouri's most historical towns, and as such, definitely worth a leisurely visit.

St. Joseph or "StJoMo" was one of the major transportation points during the heyday of the westward movement, and perhaps the most important departure point for the Oregon Trail. The westward movement began in earnest shortly after Jefferson made the Louisiana Purchase in 1803 and sent Lewis and Clark forth to see what he had bought. Traders, trappers, settlers, and assorted others followed the Missouri River due west upstream to where it makes a sharp turn north. The first route west was the Santa Fe Trail, which was created in 1821 when an enterprising man named William Becknell, of Franklin, Missouri, organized a company of teamsters and traders to haul American-made utensils and clothing to Santa Fe to sell to people who had no other access to these goods. His first trip was an enormous success, and others soon followed his wagon tracks on the 900-mile journey.

Independence and Weston were important last-chance outposts for the flood of immigrants heading west, but St. Joseph became the departure point of choice for those going to California and Oregon

Country. It wasn't long before St. Joseph was the only choice offered by steamboat companies. Part of the reason for the town's success was the business abilities of the town's founder, Joseph Robidoux. Robidoux was a St. Louis Frenchman who worked as a fur trader for the American Fur Company before deciding to go into the business of building towns. He first established a post on the creek called Roy's Branch, which became known as Robidoux's Post. He was an excellent trader, knew several native dialects, and got along well with everyone. When he built his town, named for his patron saint, he decided to have narrow medieval streets rather than broad boulevards because, he said, "I want to sell my land in lots, not give it away in streets." He also knew human nature, and when he sold lots to newcomers, he made one stipulation: Nobody could take possession of their property until he or she had harvested the hemp crop he required them to grow. In those days, hemp—marijuana to the rest of us—was used in making rope, and Robidoux was a major supplier to rope makers.

The town's longevity and dominance as a departure point to the West were guaranteed by the California gold rush of 1849. During the summer of 1849, 123 buildings appeared on Robidoux's narrow streets, and 64 of them were built of brick.

Thanks in part to the former Weston resident Ben Holladay, St. Joseph continued its dominance in the development of the West through his involvement in the short-lived Pony Express (1860–61). The company lived briefly and died quickly, but not before becoming a legend. Holladay did not own it long, and he bought it at the very end of its life, but it enabled him to become familiar with the logistics of horse-powered transportation across the West. The transcontinental telegraph lines were completed on October 24, 1861; two days later, Holladay announced that the company was closed.

The Pony Express was based at the Patee House in St. Joseph, which was built as a hotel in 1858, a sturdy brick building that covers a square block. Today the building houses the **Patee House Museum**, which includes the official **Pony Express Museum** and tells the story of Jesse James, the famous bank robber. The museum also houses a steam locomotive and mail car, the last remnants of the Hannibal & St. Joseph Railroad, which ran across the state between the two cities for which it was named. The engine is an 1880 Baldwin 4-4-0. The railroad opened in 1859 and made St. Joseph the western terminus of railroads in the U.S. This was the reason the Pony Express began in St. Joseph. Mail was sent by train to St. Joseph, and the Pony Express took over from there. Ten days later, the mail was delivered in California. Previously, it had taken up to six months for people on the West Coast to learn what had happened in the nation's capital. The Pony Express stables have been preserved to tell the story of this overromanticized and brief episode.

Next door to the Patee House is **Jesse James' house**, a small house that James, his wife Zerelda, and their children, Jesse Edwards and Mary, were renting in 1882 from a city councilman for $14 a month. After a career of bank robbery that had lasted 16 years, Jesse and his brother, Frank, had each married and their wives wanted them to settle down and live normal lives. Jesse went by the name of Tom Howard, and was indeed living quietly. But there was a $10,000 reward on his head and the temptation was too much for Bob Ford, a member of his gang. On April 3, 1882, Bob and his brother Charlie were visiting Jesse James. According to one story, James had gathered a group to plan another robbery; just after their breakfast he got up from the table to straighten a picture on the wall and Ford shot him in the back of the head. The bank robber was dead before he hit the floor. James' wife, children, and mother left the house and stayed in the Patee House for a few days before leaving town. Ford collected the reward but was portrayed as a villain for killing the man who many considered a modern-day Robin Hood (a claim never completely proven).

The killing created a political firestorm for the governor, Thomas T. Crittenden, because he had accepted money from railroads for rewards to be paid for the James boys, dead or alive. Missouri statutes set a limit of $300 of public money for rewards, but Crittenden wanted the James boys out of business, so he announced a $5,000 reward each for the arrest of Jesse and Frank, and another $5,000 if they were convicted.

Apparently, Charlie and Bob Ford made a deal with the local authorities that they would kill Jesse and surrender to the police. They did so and were quickly tried for murder, convicted, sentenced to hang, and then immediately pardoned by the governor.

Even though the James gang had murdered several people during their rampages, and certainly many more during the Civil War when they were riding with bushwhackers throughout Missouri, Arkansas, Kansas, and Oklahoma, they were still considered heroes. This is apparently where the Robin Hood legends began, even though no evidence has surfaced that the gang helped anyone other than immediate family, and themselves. The governor rode out the firestorm and Frank rode the infamy while giving his public confessionals about the evils of murdering and robbing.

Bob Ford was murdered in Creed, Colorado, and Charlie was soon killed in a barroom brawl in the Black Hills. The house Jesse was murdered in was moved to a highway and set up as a tourist attraction. In 1977 Mr. and Mrs. Robert Keatley bought it to donate to the Pony Express Historical Association, and it was moved next door to the museum.

IN THE AREA

Most of the following listings are for Weston. St. Joseph is a large city with a wide variety of hotels, B&Bs, and good restaurants.

America Bowman Restaurant, 500 Welt Street, Weston. Call 816-640-5235. A combination restaurant and local museum, the menu leans toward pub food, such as cheddar and ale soup, bangers and mash, and fish and chips.

Avalon Café, 608 Main Street, Weston. Call 816-640-2835. Serves continental cuisine.

Benner House Bed & Breakfast, 645 Main Street, Weston. Call 816-640-2616. This rambling Queen Anne home, with wraparound porches on both floors, was built by an early owner of the McCormick Distillery, followed by 80 years of ownership by the Benner family. No children or pets. Web site: www.bennerhouse.com.

Hatchery House B&B, 618 Short Street, Weston. Call 816-640-5700. This is a house with a history, which is humorously and accurately reflected in its name. It began as a nice home for a number of different owners until it was converted into a boarding house in the 1930s. Because the rent was low, many newlyweds lived there and, newlyweds being newlyweds, many families were started there. Thus, the nickname that stuck. Each room is filled with antique furniture and each room is different from the others. Web site: www.hatcherybb.com.

Laurel Brooke Farm B&B, 22520 Highway M, Weston. Call 816-640-2525. A large barn was converted by Amish craftsmen into this lavish bed-and-breakfast, situated on 40 acres just outside Weston. In addition to the usual B&B amenities, this one offers long walks through the fields. Children over 12 welcome. Web site: www.laurelbrooke farm.com

McCormick Country Store, 420 Main Street, Weston. Call 816-640-3149. In addition to McCormick whiskey, the store also sells items promoting the company and premium cigars.

The Murphy House, 926 Spring Street, Weston. Call 816-640-5577. This three-story Victorian is one of the most imposing of the homes built in the early 20th century, and has been restored to its former glory. Only two bedrooms are used for the B&B and each has a sitting room and private bath. A third bedroom is available for meetings.

National Silk Art Museum (in Charlemagne's Restaurant), 616 Thomas Street, Weston. Call 816-640-2609. More than 150 French silk tapestries based on works of major artists are on display. Artists represented include Raphael, Ruben, and David. Open Wednesday through Sunday. Free admission. Web site: www.nationalsilkart museum.com.

Orval Hixon Vaudeville Museum (in **Sundance Gallery**), 509 Main Street, Weston. Call 816-386-9925. Orval Hixon was the official Orpheum and Shubert vaudeville circuit photographer and he photographed many of the stars. These included Al Jolson, Theda Bara, Eddie Cantor, and Eddie Rickenbacker. Other photographs show various aspects of life in the Weston area from prehistoric times to World War II. Free admission.

Patee House Museum, 1202 Penn Street, St. Joseph. Call 816-232-8206. Located in a frontier hotel that was also headquarters for the Pony Express, the museum is on the National Register of Historic Places. The building also houses a steam locomotive and a railroad depot.

Pritle Winery, 502 Spring Street, Weston. Call 816-640-5728. The winery is inside a former German Lutheran Evangelical Church, with wine and picnic supplies sold in the gift shop. Web site: www.pritle winery.com.

Saint George Hotel, 502 Main Street, Weston. Call 816-640-9902. Built as a hotel in 1845 at the peak of Weston's growth, the brick hotel went through numerous ownership and usage changes before being reborn, yet again, as a hotel. Now it has 26 rooms and many amenities to make guests feel welcome and comfortable, including warm cookies, DVD players, and complimentary continental breakfast. Web site: www.thesaintgeorge.com.

The Vineyards, 505 Spring Street, Weston. Call 816-640-5588. This restaurant specializes in lamb, duck, veal, and beef tenderloin, and serves the local Pritle wines. Web site: www.thevineyards restaurant.com.

Weston Historical Museum, 601 Main Street, Weston. Call 816-386-2977. A wide variety of historical items are on display, including a pair of rare Native American moccasins, medical instruments, Civil War relics, a newspaper office, and an assortment of home furnishings and décor. The museum sponsors occasional "Cemetery Strolls into the Past," in which actors portray people from Weston's past. Closed Mondays, holidays, and from mid-December through mid-March. Free admission. Web site: www.westonhistoricalmuseum.com.

OTHER CONTACTS

Lewis and Clark State Park, Rushville. Call 816-579-5564. Web site: www.mostateparks.com/lewisandclark.htm.

St. Joseph Area Chamber of Commerce. Call 816-232-4461. Web site: www.saintjoseph.com

Snow Creek Ski Area. Call 816-640-2200. Web site: www.skisnowcreek.com

Weston Development Company. Call 816-386-2909. Web site: www.westonmo.com.

Gallatin, Jamesport, and Kirksville

Estimated length: St. Joseph to Edina, 190 miles
Estimated time: half day

Getting there: Take MO 6 from St. Joseph east to Edina.

Highlights: Gallatin and its rich history, the Amish community around **Jamesport**, the Mormon War, rolling hills, abandoned homes, and small, pretty towns. The description of this trip ends at **Edina**. However, you can continue on MO 6 to its end at the intersection with US 24, which will take you south to **Palmyra** and **Hannibal**.

MO 6 begins in downtown St. Joseph as an extension of Frederick Boulevard, ducks under US 71, and heads east across farmland. It bumps against US 36 and ricochets due north for about 10 miles, then goes back to its east–northeast direction across the dark farmlands of northern Missouri. Outside St. Joseph, the countryside is lovely, with rolling hills, rich soil, and lots of trees still standing rather than being scraped off for houses. St. Joseph ends quite abruptly, with very few signs of gentrification creeping eastward.

October is an excellent time for this drive because front porches and windows will be filled with pumpkins and goblins dressed in overalls, lounged on porch swings and draped over mailboxes in anticipation of Halloween. It seems that no self-respecting goblin or scarecrow appears in public without a red bandana. Laundry hangs from clotheslines, and if you have ever slept on sun-and-air–dried sheets and pillowcases, for a fleeting moment you will remember how much better they smell than those out of a dryer.

Gallatin has an imposing courthouse in the center of a larger-than-usual square. The town is famous in the history of the Old West for the 1883 trial of Frank James for the murder of William Westfall, a train conductor, and Frank McMillan, a passenger, during a robbery two years earlier. He was acquitted. Frank was about the only member of the James and Younger gang to have a normal life after the others died.

In one of those ironies of public life, after his acquittal Frank James helped support himself by going on the lecture circuit to preach that crime doesn't pay, although he was standing up there making his crimes pay very handsomely. The great Texas folklorist J. Frank Dobie wrote that, after his acquittal, James wore out several good horses riding them at night on a route in either Arkansas or Oklahoma, trying to remember where he had flung saddlebags containing several thousand dollars from a robbery. It was a dark night, but Frank and Jesse could hear the posse behind them. It is one of those stories we are reluctant to research in case it might not be true.

A short distance north of Gallatin is a religious shrine that is sacred to Mormons, because it was here that the Mormons stopped after being driven out of a series of towns. While Joseph Smith, the founder, was here with his followers, he announced that this spot, named **Adam-Ondi-Ahman**, was where Adam offered sacrifices to God after he and Eve were driven from the Garden of Eden.

The Mormon experience in Missouri is one of the state's darkest, meanest, and most shameful chapters. No group, religious or otherwise, was treated worse than the Mormons. They were murdered, beaten, raped, ridiculed, and harassed until they finally left the state. It is still a painful story to read because the intense hatred was so obviously based on religion and nothing else. During the 19th century especially, the religious freedom promised to immigrants was a cruel joke.

The Church of Latter-Day Saints was founded in 1830 by Joseph Smith, Oliver Cowdery, and David Whitmer in western New York State. Smith was the true founder because it was he who had the visions and the organizational skills that led to a meeting on April 6, 1830, which was described as a charismatic event. Members had visions, spoke in tongues, revealed prophesies, shouted praises, and fainted.

Once their religion gained some power, Mormons became unwelcome in New York, in part because of their aggressive recruiting efforts. In addition, they fought for power among themselves as they struggled to grow. The basic teachings Smith related to the others were followed in general, but they were also general enough for various interpretations. This also did not lead to cohesiveness.

In 1831 the Church moved its headquarters to Kirtland, Ohio, because a former Campbellite minister, Sidney Rigdon, converted to Mormonism and his congregation followed, thus making these new converts the largest group of Mormons. Smith and Rigdon founded a bank for members but it failed and they lost several members to a splinter group as a result. This schism was part of the reason Mormons appeared in northern Missouri in the early 1830s. At first they were welcomed, and the state created Caldwell County specifically for the Mormons. The county seat was a town called Far West.

The first conflicts with other Missourians came when the Mormons began expanding into neighboring counties. At the same time, the Mormons were fighting among themselves. The events that followed are known as the Mormon War, and it indeed fit every definition of a war. If any Missourian did not believe the country could easily sink into a civil war three decades later, they would have to be unaware of the viciousness of the Mormon War.

Mobs were easy to assemble to go against the Mormons, particularly those Mormons who had ventured outside the Caldwell County lines. The Mormons were not simply beaten. They were murdered. Their houses were burned to the ground and all their possessions stolen, and their farm animals stolen or slaughtered. The women were raped. Children were murdered. Sometimes the Mormons weren't murdered but were tarred and feathered, which was one of the cruelest forms of torture and popular during that period. Heavy oil or paving tar was heated to the boiling point, then poured on the victim; feathers were then flung on him or her and became embedded in the tar.

Many people died of the severe burns this caused, and all survivors were scarred for life.

The Mormon War was total war of the scorched-earth variety. The Mormons owed more to the Old Testament than the New Testament in their beliefs, and if they turned the other cheek to an enemy and were still attacked, it would happen only one time. They fought back fiercely, but they were vastly outnumbered and out-armed. They didn't stand a chance.

It was during this war that Alexander Doniphan first showed his strength of character and his skills as a leader when he not only refused an order to slaughter a group of Mormons under arrest, but also threatened the officer who gave that order. The complete story is in the profile of Doniphan in Chapter 8.

The Mormons lost the war, and they were forced out of Missouri. In keeping with the scorched-earth philosophy, once they were gone all traces of their religion were torn down and burned and the property turned into farmland. Their county seat of Far West was completely destroyed and now corn grows where the town once stood. Not a trace of it was permitted to remain. A sign marks the site of Adam-Ondi-Ahman on the Grand River between Gallatin and Jameson. It is a very modest sign.

The state of Illinois took the Mormons in, and in 1939 they established headquarters in Navoo. The leaders held in prison in Missouri eventually escaped, and in 1841 they began building a temple in Navoo. The infighting continued, and when Joseph Smith organized a secret council that proclaimed Smith as Prophet, Priest, and King, and made polygamy legal, a local newspaper found out and planned to release the details of the council. So Smith had the newspaper office destroyed.

The internal warfare continued, but this also had the odd effect of making the religion stronger; its members were more determined to survive, even though the Church kept splitting into splinter groups. The state of Illinois grew tired of dealing with the Church and the locals around Navoo began fighting with its members. Finally, the new leader, Brigham Young, decided enough was enough and told the church members that they must leave. The majority of members decided to follow Brigham Young and the other leaders on a trek west to seek new lands. They arrived in the Salt Lake Valley in 1847.

Sign for tourists at Jamesport

Religion is a dominant feature on this trip across the top of Missouri. After surviving the Mormon area, you next come to **Jamesport**, which is in the heart of **Amish country**. They have not participated in any wars, and are surviving very well in the black dirt and rolling hills of the region.

If you don't see horse-drawn wagons or farm equipment, the first clue of where you are might well be the beautifully tended farmhouses and barns, with no electrical power or telephone lines leading in from the main lines along the highway. Chances are, however, you will meet and pass the distinctive enclosed black buggies pulled by one horse and decorated with a vivid orange triangle on back to alert drivers.

The third clue comes at the edge of Jamesport. A large red sign states JAMESPORT, and beneath that is the information that you will find maps and restrooms at City Hall. To the right of the sign is a large, black silhouette of an Amish wagon and horse.

The Amish came to the Jamesport area from Ohio and Pennsylvania in the 1950s during one of their periodic migrations, which occur for a variety of reasons: when their communities become too crowded and too inbred, when they find more reasonably priced

Amish farmer plowing with seven-horse spring-tooth harrow

farmland, when the governmental regulations are too restrictive, or when they are taken to court for some infraction or disagreement. The Amish do not defend themselves in court. Sometimes Amish are expelled from the community for breaking the rules.

The most noticeable aspect of the Amish religion is that they do not believe in modern conveniences, such as electricity, telephones, and fuel-powered equipment. The wheel is the major technological innovation they permit, but little beyond that. They make their own clothing, grow most of their own food, and rely on their community for most assistance. Their religion does not permit photographs of its members, so the Jamesport Chamber of Commerce makes a point of telling visitors not to photograph them.

The Amish do not have the ideal life that some people think. They have all the problems shared by humankind, except those created by technology. They have family troubles, worries about income, and all the normal fears. In addition, because of generations of cousins marrying, some genetic problems have become magnified. The Amish have a high percentage of dwarfism, a high incidence of twins, and metabolic problems. It has been pointed out that five surnames account for about half of the Amish population. There seems to be no solution for the gene pool problem because very few people join the order, so the anomalies will naturally continue.

The religious order began in Switzerland when a group led by Jacob Ammann broke away from the Mennonites. The Amish believe in separation from the world and do not go to war, swear oaths, or hold public office. They hold religious meetings in homes and they limit education to the eighth grade.

The Amish presence has helped make Jamesport one of Missouri's most rural-looking towns. At last count, Jamesport had a population of less than 600, but it supported 16 antique shops, 26 specialty shops (selling quilts, dolls, rugs, crafts, and so on), and two companies that specialize in tours of the Amish community. Two stores a short distance south of town are owned by the Amish: one, a bulk-food store, and the other specializing in their preferred fabrics for clothing, linen, curtains, and other uses.

The identity brought by the Amish has helped keep the town from fading away entirely. Before 1925 Jamesport had a population of more than 5,000 and was the busiest railroad town between Chicago and Kansas City; an average of 40 trains went through daily. It was also the largest shipping port in Missouri. Now it is a combination farm town and tourist destination. Several festivals are held throughout the year, and guided tours take visitors through the town and out into the countryside to call on Amish families.

Jamesport is also the hometown of Aurand Harris, the playwright of several of America's most-produced children's plays. Harris wrote *Punch and Judy* and the musical adaptation of *Androdes and the Lion*, among many other plays.

After leaving Jamesport, MO 6 heads northeast along the hills and valleys into **Trenton**, another of those neatly arranged towns you come to expect in areas with good farmland. The town has a population of about 6,000 and lots of brick houses, a distinctive courthouse with a tall steeple, and other equally impressive public buildings. Because of its impressive buildings, Trenton bears a slightly European look.

The Thompson River, a fair-size stream, flows through the edge of town, but it isn't long before you cross NO CREEK. That's what the sign says. It is one of those questions best left unanswered because of the danger that the answer will be much less interesting than the question.

Does its name mean there is no creek there at all—just a dry bed? Maybe somebody said "no" to somebody beside the creek. Or does it represent denial of some dastardly deed? It remains one of life's minor mysteries.

From Trenton, the highway winds its way through more and more timber—oak and pine with thickets of blackberries and sumac. By now you will be accustomed to the slap-slap of your tires hitting the joints of the concrete highways of the region. The towns are small but well tended, except for an occasional church needing a coat of paint, which could mean that the congregation has shifted its allegiance to another church. Things like that happen.

After **Gait, Humphrey,** and **Reger**, and hundreds of acres of hay fields dotted with round bales, **Milan** appears. This is the Sullivan County seat, a pretty town of about 1,700, with several old, comfortable homes and an unhurried look about it.

Next comes **Green City**, a crossroads town with an airport named Richard Widmark Airport. Richard Widmark? It turns out that the actor once was a partner in a cattle feedlot in Green City, and when he came to check on his investment, he landed his plane at the local airport. The airport needed a longer runway, so Widmark donated enough land to make the extension possible. The locals showed their gratitude by naming the airport for him.

The timber becomes thicker as you continue to drive eastward, and many fencerows are marked with trees as well as posts and wire. The last town before **Kirksville** is **Novinger**, which has about 500 residents now but once was a major coal-mining area. The **Coal Miners Museum** tells this part of its history, and the **Isaac and Samuel Novinger Log Home** is a two-story home built about 1848, which has been restored by a local organization.

As you near Kirksville, the number of trophy houses increases. Most have white-gravel drives leading to them, usually winding rather than straight, as though a *feng shui* consultant came and went after designing the driveway, because the large houses have little or no greenery around them. It is as though the owners want to be certain the house is all we see.

With a population of about 18,000, Kirksville is the major town in this part of Missouri. It has Northeast Missouri State University and an old, unpretentious, and friendly downtown district built around an old-fashioned square. The downtown buildings are old but not worn out, and when you ask people for directions, they'll stop what they are doing, look you in the eye, and take their time to be sure you understand them.

From Kirksville, you can continue on MO 6 to the Mississippi River by turning south on MO 24 to **Palmyra** and onward to **Hannibal**. For the purposes of the routes selected for this book, this chapter ends at **Edina**, whereas the following chapter takes you due south to **Bethel**.

IN THE AREA

Brashear House Bed and Breakfast, 1318 E. Normal Street, Kirksville. Call 660-627-0378. This 1905 Colonial house with a wraparound porch is across the street from Brashear Park and is loaded with memorabilia and antiques. Four suites. Web site: www.brashearhouse.com.

Coal Miners Museum (Novinger Isaac and Samuel Novinger Log Home). The log homestead from about 1850 includes the two-story log cabin, a barn and smokehouse. Call 816-488-5280.

Cottage Grove Bed and Breakfast, 301 S. Cottage Grove Avenue, Kirksville. Call 660-627-4444. Ranch-style home in the country with four bedrooms. Web site: www.cottagegrovebnb.com.

Hyde Mansion Bed and Breakfast, 418 E. 7th Street, Trenton. Call 660-359-5631. Six rooms, each with private bath. Children over 12 welcome.

OTHER CONTACTS

Jamesport Community Association. Call 816-684-6146. Web site: www.jamesportmo.com

Kirksville Area Chamber of Commerce. Call 816-665-3766. Web site: www.kirksvillechamber.com.

St. Joseph Area Chamber of Commerce. Call 816-232-4461 (also for information on **Gallatin**). Web site: www.saintjoseph.com.

Trenton Area Chamber of Commerce. Call 816-359-4324. Web site: www.trentonmochamber.com.

CHAPTER 3

Edina to Bethel

Estimated length: 30 miles
Estimated time: 45 minutes

Getting there: From MO 6 at Edina, take MO 15 south through Novelty and Plevna to Bethel, then on to Shelbyville, Paris, and Mexico, or east to Hannibal.

Highlights: Bethel, with its unique Oregon Trail story; **Paris**, with its many historical buildings, including the **Mark Twain's birthplace**; and the **Union Covered Bridge**.

If you need a reason other than visiting **Bethel** for taking MO 15 south from Edina, here's a good one: to see **Novelty** and **Cherry Box**. These towns show on the map but mostly exist only in local memory. Still, they appear on maps and if you don't study the map carefully, you will drive past them and find yourself in Bethel, a small town with a big story to tell.

Bethel is one of the most thoroughly studied towns in the state. It compares well with Hermann as a cornerstone of the German immigrants' experience in Missouri, but Bethel is a clear winner in the

This is one of several false-front business buildings in Bethel that was surviving the slow depopulation of northern Missouri as people moved to larger towns.

"eccentricity" sweepstakes. It was founded in 1845 by a Prussian immigrant named Wilhelm Keil who, with his wife Louise, came to America in 1835, the same year a few religious leaders in both Europe and America predicted that Christ would return to earth. The Keils lived in New York for a while, then Pennsylvania, then Ohio. Keil was a charismatic man; after he had been in America a while, he became an ordained preacher, then left organized religion to start his own brand of Christian communism. He sometimes led people to believe he was the Messiah; detractors didn't say he exactly told them he was the Messiah, but he never denied it when asked. Keil was obviously one of those leaders who can always find people who are so disappointed with their lives that they will follow without question someone who looks them in the eye and tells them they'll take good care of them.

Keil's followers were not stupid people, however. When he organized his Society of Bethel, the commune became enormously wealthy. Not only did the members do well as farmers, with communal crops and livestock, but they also built a glove factory, a whiskey distillery, a wagon shop, and a tool factory. They built the best plows in that part of Missouri. They settled in northeast Missouri on the banks of the North River, which flows east into the Mississippi some 40 miles away. They named their town Bethel, then they spread out in the area and established the nearby towns of Hebron, Elim, Mamri, and Nineveh, north of Kirksville, which was later changed to Connelsville.

The colony did so well that, by the time the great migration to the Oregon Country began, Keil wanted to spread his community and its teachings to this new land. This is what led to one of the strangest stories from the American frontier. Keil sent some members of his group to the Oregon Country with a wagon train to search for a place to establish a new colony. They came back a year or so later with the recommendation that the colony be established on the broad and beautiful—but perpetually damp—land bordering Willapa Bay, just north of the Columbia River. They reasoned that the often stormy and deadly Columbia River bar was more of a barrier than an avenue of trade, and that Willapa Bay, with its protected waters, would become the major port, and that railroads and highways would transport goods around the mouth of the Columbia.

Thus armed with information and a destination, Keil decided to lead the group of pilgrims himself, and he left his son August in charge of the Bethel colony. The strong leadership genes of the father did not pass down to this son, however, and although residents were said to be personally fond of August, in later years they noted that he was often drunk.

Keil set the spring of 1855 as the departure date. Perhaps it was partly because that date would be exactly 20 years after his arrival in the United States and exactly 10 years after he led the establishment of the communities in Missouri, headquartered in Bethel.

Another son, Wilhelm, Jr. or "Willie," was appointed to go along with his father, and he was excited about the prospect. Then the 19-year-old youth fell ill with malaria, one of the most dreaded diseases of the period. Malaria was one of the primary reasons that families and communities left the Midwest and Southeast for the Oregon Country.

When young Willie fell ill, everyone assumed he would die long before the departure date of May 23, 1855. He did, but in lucid periods during his brief illness he pleaded with his father to take him along. When Willie became delirious from the fever, he imagined himself leading the wagon train across the prairies and the mountains to that cool, green, clean land at the edge of the continent. His father promised Willie he would indeed go with them, and before the boy died Keil ordered that a special wagon be built for him. It carried a tank into which the boy's body was placed; then the tank was filled with alcohol to preserve the body until their arrival at their new home on Willapa Bay.

From Bethel to Willapa Bay, legend and fact become intermingled, but the story of Wilhelm Keil is already so off center that we might as well believe everything that has been written. The best version is that Willie did lead the wagon train across the continent because Keil ordered the hearse to be the lead wagon all the way. The best version also states that the Native Americans along the way heard of the hearse leading a wagon train and were afraid of it, and that when a band of natives who hadn't heard of the strange procession drove away several head of the Bethelites' cattle, other Native Americans, who knew the story, forced the thieves to return the cattle.

This makes for good reading, and it could well be true. At least the basic facts are correct. The Bethel wagon train consisted of 35 wagons and about 175 people. It has been written that the Bethelites were the wealthiest group to cross the plains. When the wagon train reached

Union Covered Bridge

Willapa Bay, one of the first tasks was to give Willie a decent burial. A site was chosen a short distance inland on a knoll overlooking the Willapa River, not far from where it enters the bay. There the grave remains today, protected by Washington's smallest state park.

The trip across the country fed Keil's messianic opinion of himself, and he sent epistles back to his followers. An excerpt from one letter reads:

> *The whole desert cried out that we should perish here. . . . There was nothing for us to do but proceed from sunrise to the setting sun, and curst this region of hell and death. I gave orders that no wagon should be left behind, and declared that I meant to take my people through the desert even if all the seven princes*

of darkness should oppose us. I did get all our people and wag-
ons through and the devil was put to shame. We met hundreds
of Indians at Salmon Falls who were glad to see my face. I had
power over the Indians and could do with them whatever I
wanted to do.

Keil and his group weren't impressed with the town site on Willapa
Bay after all. They knew it would not be a good place for their business interests, and they were right. Willapa Bay never developed as a
port, except as a place to ship logs to Asia. The bay has no large towns,
and the major commercial enterprises around it are timber, oyster
farming, cranberries, and tourism.

After looking around the Northwest at some length, Keil settled
on a town site south of Portland overlooking the Willamette River. He
named this settlement Aurora, for his daughter, who would die in
1864 of smallpox. He and his group remained in Aurora until Keil died
in 1877.

Over the next dozen years, other groups of Bethelites migrated to
the Oregon Country: 42 wagons in 1863, 11 in 1865, 15 in 1867. Others
came by ship around Cape Horn until more than 600 had emigrated
from Missouri. The dream of Christian communism died with Keil,
and two years after his death the community divided everything into
personal property and went about their lives much as their neighbors.
The same thing happened in Bethel.

Many of Bethel's original homes and public buildings are still
standing, including the post office, the community hall where visitors
slept, the bandstand, and some store buildings. One of the five hand-
dug wells is still used. The entire town is a **National Historic Site**, and
hosts numerous social events throughout the year, including the
Harvest Fest in October.

The drive south from Bethel is through more rolling hills and rich
farmland, and lots of timber, which is spotted here and there in draws,
on a few hilltops, and along fencerows.

The next town is **Paris**, which has several points of interest, even
though it has fewer than 2,000 residents. It is the birthplace of **Samuel
L. Clemens**, better known as Mark Twain. The two-room cabin in
which Missouri's most famous writer was born is now a museum. A
short distance away is **Mark Twain State Park**.

Paris also has a **Norman Rockwell** connection: the artist came to Paris and painted a series on the theme of a country newspaper editor. He used the editor's office as his location and employees of the Monroe County Appeal as models for the series.

Nine miles southwest of Paris (take MO 24 west 5 miles, then Route C west for 0.25 mile) is the **Union Covered Bridge**, which was built in 1871 across the Elk Fork of the Salt River. The bridge is 125 feet long and approximately 17 feet wide. It was built for $5,000 and is still in good shape. However, it is virtually impossible to photograph because brush has grown up around it. Photos from the side are likely to reveal an unidentifiable white slab of something in the trees. Photographing the bridge head-on is equally unsatisfying because it looks as though it could be a barn door or a façade.

To get back to the main road, take Route AA east and watch for signs aiming you down a narrow road that leads back to MO 15. This route ends in **Mexico**, a bustling town of about 12,000. Mexico is known for its American Saddle Horses, a breed popular in the area. The **Audrain Historical and American Saddle Horse Museum** displays artifacts relating to the breed. At one time, Mexico was the major fire-clay brick manufacturing place in America. Almost every brick used in Missouri for buildings and streets came from Mexico, thanks to an enormous deposit of clay found beneath the town.

From Mexico, you can continue south on US 54 to the Missouri River, or drive east to the Mississippi River to explore MO 79, part of the **Great River Road** that runs from Hannibal to St. Louis.

IN THE AREA

Bethel Fest Hall Bed and Breakfast, Bethel. Call 314-284-6493. This B&B has a café downstairs, which is the only place to eat and sleep on this short trip—you will probably want to keep driving. The fest hall is a very old and worn building and the rooms are plain, with sagging beds. The Bethel German Colony headquarters are in the same building, one of the few businesses still functioning in this dying town.

OTHER CONTACTS

Mexico Area Chamber of Commerce. Call 314-581-2765. Web site: www.mexico-chamber.org.

The Lost Art of Front-Porch Sitting

All across Missouri you see front porches, but seldom will you see anyone sitting on them. Many of these lifeless porches have kitchen chairs, rocking chairs, and swings on them, but they sit silently, moving only when a strong wind blows. Sitting on front porches is a fading memory so distant that many middle-aged people have never seen anyone sitting on porches in the evening, and certainly have never done so themselves.

There was a time, at least until the 1950s, when nearly every front porch was populated: by women shelling peas, peeling apples, mending clothing, chatting, or reading. Children would be scattered around the porch, out in the front yard, or down the street with neighbors. When the man of the house came home from the fields or work in town, the family would migrate inside for supper (in most porch societies, the evening meal was always called "supper" while dinner was "the noon meal"). After supper, the family would wander back out to the front porch to watch the sunset and the arrival of lightning bugs, and to catch the cool breezes night sometimes brought.

All the while, everyone in the neighborhood would be socializing. You could see a neighbor coming home in a grouchy mood, and you could tell where a woman had been shopping that day. Women gave each other permanents on the porch. Go for a walk and you would most likely speak to someone from every household sitting on each front porch on your route. Sometimes you would interrupt the walk to go out back to see a neighbor's yard, or to see how the boy was doing building his soapbox derby car, which had displaced the family car in the garage. This kind of interaction is not nearly as likely to happen today because most people either stay inside their houses or go into their backyards, which usually are a continuation of the privacy of the house.

Front porches are peculiar to the United States. No European homes have ever had them. Some believe they were adapted from the tiny cabins built by black slaves and former slaves in the Caribbean. There is also evidence that a 19th-century landscaper named Andrew Jackson Downing began promoting porches as a way to make architecture here different from that in Europe.

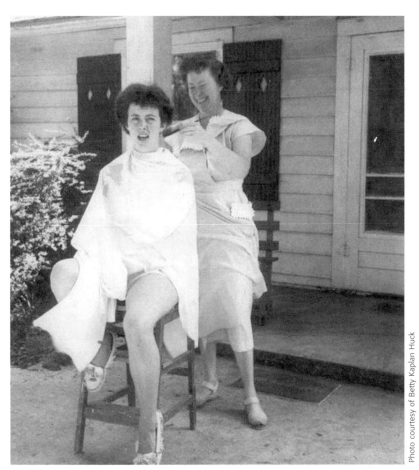

Photo courtesy of Betty Kaplan Huck

Betty Kaplan getting a haircut from her mother, Verda Doron Kaplan, on the front steps of their Raytown home, so hair wouldn't have to be swept off the front porch, 1952.

Many Americans are nostalgic for porches and organizations have been formed to celebrate them. One is the Professional Porch Sitters Union. It doesn't have a motto, just an invitation: "Sit down a spell. That can wait."

Those among us fortunate enough to remember the culture of the front porch will also remember sitting on the swing with a boy or girl in the gathering darkness, while the parents were inside reading or listening to the radio. No matter what they were doing, that special hearing capacity all parents have was at work. The least change in the squeaking of the swing brought an inquiring adult to the front door or window.

It seems a pity that we have let television move us inside and out of constant contact with our neighbors. Few activities are more soothing to the soul than sitting on a rocking chair or a porch swing and moving slowly back and forth, letting the day end peacefully and painlessly.

Along the Great River Road

Estimated length: 120 miles
Estimated time: 3 hours

Getting there: From Hannibal, head south on MO 79 through Louisiana, to I-70 just outside St. Louis.

Highlights: The **Mississippi River** and barge traffic, the Mark Twain town of **Hannibal, Louisiana** and its beautiful homes and park overlooking the Mississippi, old towns and villages along the river.

Although the **Great River Road** in Missouri begins on the Iowa state line and goes through several towns before disappearing in the traffic of St. Louis, this stretch of the **Mississippi River** is dominated by one man and the many characters and events of which he wrote. The man was Samuel Langhorne Clemens, alias Mark Twain (1835–1910). This entire corner of the state is referred to as Mark Twain Country. It is doubtful that anyone else who ever lived in Missouri was as universally loved as he, although it took a few Hannibal citizens a while to forgive him for a few things he said.

Clemens wasn't a big man, but his alter ego, Mark Twain, casts a shadow across Missouri as long as that of Harry S. Truman. For most

Georgia Street in the town of Louisiana has retained its 19th century look.

Mark Twain Home and Museum in Hannibal

Americans, and millions elsewhere, Mark Twain and the Mississippi River are so tightly intermingled that without him the river would be big and muddy, and not much else. It certainly wouldn't hold that romance for people all over the world, and we wouldn't be so likely to look at the river and dream of floating down it on a raft.

Mark Twain is the best thing that ever happened to **Hannibal**. Without him, Hannibal would be no more famous than its neighboring town to the south, Louisiana, or Keokuk, Illinois, to the north. There aren't many towns in America more closely identified with one of its citizens: John Steinbeck and Monterey, California; Thomas Wolfe and Asheville, North Carolina; and only a few others come to mind, but none of these links is as strong as that of Twain and Hannibal.

Not only is Twain important to Hannibal, but he is also generally credited with creating the American novel when he wrote *The Adventures of Tom Sawyer*. Despite the dark undertones of this novel and its companion, *The Adventures of Huckleberry Finn*, Twain is also considered America's greatest humorist.

Hannibal nurtures its relationship with Twain as much as it can, and this relationship is the town's major industry. An average of 250,000 people visit Hannibal each year. Nearly every event through-

Riverboat with towboat in background in Hannibal

out the year is somehow tied to Twain and the characters in his books. There is a **Huck Finn Shopping Center** west of town and **Mark Twain Lake** farther west of town. **Cardiff Hill** was so named because Twain once said it reminded him of the hills in Cardiff, Wales. The part of US 36 that goes through town is called Mark Twain Avenue. There is an **Injun Joe Campground**, the **Mark Twain Outdoor Theater**, and the **Mark Twain Cave and Campground**. There are also **Sawyer's Creek Fun Park and Christmas Shop**, the **riverboat** *Mark Twain*, a tour named **Twainland Express** with a pseudo-locomotive, and a horse-drawn wagon ride called the **Mark Twain Clopper**. There is a shop named **Aunt Polly's Handcrafts** and a restaurant named **Huck's Homestead**.

Each Fourth of July marks the end of the weeklong **National Tom Sawyer Days**, which feature a national fence-painting contest, a jumping frog contest, Tomboy Sawyer contests, and pie-eating contests. There is also a mud volleyball game on the Fourth of July, and hotels usually post signs at the door to keep out these particular athletes.

The house that Twain grew up in, which is two blocks up the hill from the town's gigantic grain elevators, was recently restored. It has exhibits that include a lock of Twain's hair, and photos from his life and of people on whom he based his characters. His mother became Aunt Polly, Laura Hawkins, a next-door neighbor, became Becky Thatcher, and Tom Blankenship was Huck Finn. Upstairs is Tom's room, with the window he climbed out of to meet Huck. Adjoining the home is the **Mark Twain Museum**, with many mementos, including rare first editions of his numerous books, one of his white suits, some of his favorite pipes, and one of his desks.

Next door is **Becky Thatcher's house**, which has been turned into a bookstore on the main floor, with two rooms upstairs decorated in period furnishings.

Another Clemens home is the **1830 Pilaster House**, in which the Clemens family lived for about a year after Twain's father, an attorney, became so debt-ridden that they had to move out of their home. A statue of Tom and Huck is at the foot of Cardiff Hill and, on the crest, is the lighthouse built in 1935 to honor Twain. The town has many more Twain connections, in names of shops, businesses, confections, gifts, and articles of clothing. It all seems to work for everyone.

The river route continues south from Hannibal alongside MO 79, an honest-to-goodness country highway with only two lanes, lots of double yellow lines, blind curves, modest farmhouses, blackberry vines in fencerows, and thickets you just know are sheltering coveys of quail. Off to the left, never far away, is the great Mississippi River, oozing ever southward with its load of Midwestern silt. Sometimes you can see the river through the trees, which means that you'll see much more of it—and the river traffic—in winter when the trees are stripped of leaves.

The old stern-wheelers and paddle wheelers with their steam engines and whistles, have their own charm, but most people are more interested in the barges and towboats that work the Mississippi. These boats are built for the task at hand, not for looks, and they are enormously powerful. They push barges strung together for what looks like a quarter of a mile, so heavily loaded they seem to be sinking.

The first town south of Hannibal on MO 79 is **Louisiana**, one of the most beautiful on the route. It is a stately town built on the bluffs high above the river. The town has won at least one award for its well-maintained collection of Victorian business buildings. It has mansions

Mississippi River seen from viewpoint on MO 79

on the bluff overlooking the US 54 bridge that crosses the river. A small park amid the mansions affords great views, as does the park down at river level, with a high stone wall and steps leading to the water.

Although Louisiana doesn't do a lot to promote itself as a tourist destination, it recently hung beautiful banners, with a historic homes theme, through the downtown district, and at least three of its old mansions have been turned into bed-and-breakfasts.

About 10 miles downriver on MO 79 is **Clarksville**, also built along the steep bluffs, but not so high that it entirely escaped the floods of 1992–93. Clarksville has a gondola to a high hill nearby, and several B&Bs. The last of the locks and dams on the river, prosaically named **Lock and Dam No. 24**, has a viewing platform; the lake behind the dam created a habitat for the bald eagles that frequent the area. As a result, each winter the town hosts **Eagle Days,** with the cooperation of the Missouri Department of Conservation.

MO 79 continues its graceful, two-lane winding ways along the river, usually sticking to the bluffs but occasionally dropping down into the bottomland. Traffic is irregular along here. Sometimes it's bumper to bumper; other times you'll go for several miles before meeting another traveler. The road goes through towns such as **Annada,** which has grain elevators beside the railroad track, and **Elsberry,** which has a large nursery with ornamental trees on hills beside the highway. **Winfield,** which has a ferry over to Illinois, is a junky and funky little town beside the highway.

Southward from Winfield, the traffic increases; the highway moves away from the river and is soon gobbled up by I-70 at **O'Fallon.**

IN THE AREA

Including the three listed here, there are about 20 hotels, motels, and bed-and-breakfasts in Hannibal, so you will have a wide variety of places to investigate before your visit.

Applegate Bed and Breakfast, 7328 Frankfort Road, Louisiana. Call 573-754-4322. This is an 1850s farmhouse outside of town where you can enjoy hiking and tennis.

Belle's Secret, 111 Bird Street, Hannibal. Call 573-221-6662. This one is in a renovated bank building in the heart of town and walking distance to everything. It has four suites with a Jacuzzi in each. Web site: www.lulabelles.com.

Eagle's Nest Inn, 221 Georgia Street, Louisiana. Call 573-754-9888. A former bank building, the inn has seven guestrooms, all with private baths. It is a block from the Mississippi and offers a bistro, a winery, restaurant, and gift shop. Web site: www.theeaglesnest-louisiana.com.

Garth Woodside Mansion B&B, 11069 New London Road, Hannibal. Call 888-427-8409. This mansion, built in 1871, has been turned into a large (eight guest rooms) B&B out in the country on a 39-acre estate. Children over 13 welcome with prior arrangement. No pets. Web site: www.garthmansion.com.

The Great Escape Bed and Breakfast, 702 Georgia Street, Louisiana. Call 573-754-3222. A two-story Victorian home in the downtown area with a kitchen guests are free to use. A licensed massage therapist is available.

Stone School Inn Bed and Breakfast, 5388 Marlon Country Road, Hannibal. Call 573-405-0398. Built of limestone as a schoolhouse in 1834, the durable building has been turned into a B&B with two guest rooms, a card room, and exercise room. Lunch and dinner are also served. A dog named Daisy is listed as the official greeter. Web site: www.hannibal.net/visit/stoneschoolinn.

OTHER CONTACTS

Hannibal Convention and Visitors Bureau. Call 573-221-2477. Web site: www.visithannibal.com.

Louisiana Chamber of Commerce. Call 573-754-5921. Web site: www.louisiana-mo.com.

Earthquake Country

Estimated length: 65 miles
Estimated time: 3 hours to all day

Getting there: Take I-55 south from Sikeston to MO 80 east, drive through East Prairie to a spot on the map called Thirty-four Corner at the intersection of MO 80 and MO 77. Go south on MO 77 to Towosahgy State Historic Site. Continue south on MO 77 to the Dorena Ferry landing. From the ferry landing, return to the first intersection, which will be Route A. This road goes past Seven Island Conservation Area, worth a stop for a stroll on the levee. Route A leads to MO 102. Follow it a short distance north to the entrance to Big Oak Tree State Park. After hiking on the boardwalk among the giant oaks, go south on MO 102 to the first junction, which will be MO 520. Turn right (or west) and it soon becomes Route WW, which will take you into New Madrid.

Highlights: This loop trip will take most of a day to do properly. You will see some of the rich bottomland along the Mississippi River and the system of levees built by the Corps of Engineers for flood control. You will also see a once-fortified **Native American village**, with sev-

State champion bur oak, Big Oak Tree State Park

eral earthen mounds intact, and a **grove of the tallest oak trees in America**. The loop ends at **New Madrid**, epicenter of North America's strongest recorded earthquake.

This area—only a short distance down the Mississippi from where the Ohio enters—is one of the most geologically distinct areas along the entire river. Here the river has formed a peninsula that, on maps, looks like an upside-down appendix. This causes a small piece of Missouri to protrude over into Illinois and Kentucky before the river turns southwest and almost completes a circle, once again continuing its ooze southward. This bulge contains three places of interest to anthropologists, botanists, and geologists, and all three sites are very close together and can be visited easily in one drive.

Towosahgy State Historic Site is a 64-acre tract that contains one of the best-preserved **Osage Indian villages**. Its name means "old town" in the Osage language; carbon dating shows that the town was inhabited for about 400 years, beginning around the year 1000.

Unlike many of their relatives who roamed over much of Missouri, these Osage were urban folk and didn't leave the area except perhaps to trade. The town was fortified by a wall of timber, which surrounded the earthen mounds they built. The village had six of these mounds, the largest of which was 250 feet long, 180 feet wide, and stood about 16 feet high. Wooden structures were built on them and plastered over with clay and mud.

Similar mounds were common throughout much of the middle Mississippi valley. The largest and best known are the **Cahokia Mounds**, directly across the Mississippi from St. Louis, near East St. Louis. The purpose of the mounds isn't known exactly, although religious ceremonies and fortification sites are high on the list of possibilities. Archaeologists working on this puzzle once conducted an experiment and used students and volunteers as a labor pool, having them construct a mound using tools similar to those of the Mound Builders. They found that the mounds could be built in a surprisingly short time.

The Towosahgy site has produced some surprises for archaeologists. In 1970 they found remains of a tower, or bastion, and determined that more probably existed around the stockade. They found evidence that the inhabitants dug down several inches to make their floors, and that garbage pits were dug beside each house site. In these pits was evidence of the natives' diet of corn, beans, persimmons, wild plums, and deer. Not much else is known of these people because the site had been abandoned more than a century before the first Europeans came to the area, and the first archaeologists didn't begin arriving until toward the end of the 19th century.

It is a pity that more isn't known about this group of Osage, because the Osage had one of the most highly developed nations of Native Americans. The Europeans were fascinated by the Osage because they were well organized, proud, and some of the most handsome of all Native Americans. They were physically impressive and took much pride in their appearance and physical conditioning. It was said that Osage men thought nothing of walking 60 miles in a day. Consequently, they were great travelers, for trading and sometimes out of sheer curiosity. They also went on long journeys to raid other tribes.

The Osage were well organized, with an economy based on hunting, gathering, and farming. They planted crops of corn, beans, pumpkins, and squash in the spring, and then took off on hunting expeditions during the summer months without bothering to fence or guard their crops. They dried much of the meat from animals they had killed, and when they returned in the late summer, they harvested the crops and hung part of this food to dry, too. In the fall they gathered nuts and wild fruits.

The Osage were noted for their height: most men were 6 feet tall or more. Nearly every European who encountered them was impressed with their physical appearance, their personal cleanliness, and their air of confidence. The Osage didn't think much of the Europeans, however, because these men, who lived on the fringe of society, often had matted and filthy hair, wore stinking clothing, and were generally disgusting to a people who took cleanliness so seriously that they plucked much of their body hair. The Osage were so obsessed with body size and appearance that they tried several methods of making their children tall. One was to flatten the backs of babies' heads so that the head would be an inch or two taller than normal.

But before we give the Osage "noble savage" status, it is wise to remember that, although they were nice to look at, they were still people, no better or worse than any other group of people on earth. Like most Native Americans all over the continent, the Osage were slave traders long before the Europeans imported Africans. They frequently raided other tribes to capture new slaves to use in their own bands or to sell to other tribes. They usually raped the women they captured and reared the resulting children as their own. They became full-scale middlemen after the arrival of the Europeans, and captured Native American slaves for the French slave market that operated at the mouth of the Arkansas River.

The Osage also had an unusual approach to marriage, and it was closely tied to their concept of manhood and desire to improve their tribe. When a family selected a young warrior to marry a daughter, a four-day wedding would follow—a very formal, stylized function involving tattooing and various religious ceremonies. Once the marriage was consummated, the warrior then inherited all the bride's sisters, who also became his wives so that he could spread his valuable seed among a multitude of partners rather than only one. In this way, the Osage practiced selective breeding to ensure that the characteristics they liked would be perpetuated.

This practice had a cruel downside. With one man taking care of several women, the other young men who had not passed the difficult tests of manhood were forced to spend their lives without wives. They became what the Europeans called squaw men; they were forced to dress like women, they did the work of women, and they were required to live a life of celibacy so that their presumably weak genes would not be passed along to the next generation.

However, to their credit, the Osage did not succumb to liquor. After they had seen the effects of drunkenness, they wanted no part of it. Nor were they impressed with the Europeans' possessions. An old chief named Big Soldier expressed sadness for his friend George Sibley, who commanded Fort Osage for many years. "You are surrounded by slaves," the chief told him. "Everything about you is in chains, and you are in chains yourselves. I fear if I should change my pursuit for yours, I too, should become a slave."

The Osage were one of the many tribes later moved to reservations in Kansas and Oklahoma. Not understanding the concept of land ownership or exactly how their people could be uprooted from their traditional land, the Osage tribe sold its Missouri, and then its Kansas holdings. They were left with no land to call their own. Ironically, the Osage were among the Oklahoma Native Americans who became wealthy when oil was discovered on their land. Today they live on in Missouri only through some geographic names they left behind, the Towosahgy site, and a scattering of other reminders of their presence.

Only a short drive away from Towosahgy on MO 102, **Big Oak Tree State Park** covers 1,000 acres of one of the few remaining stands of virgin timber in the Mississippi bottoms. Vast forests of gigantic timber were leveled during the pioneer years, when levees were built to drain the swamps for farming and logging. This started about the turn of the 19th century. When the New Madrid earthquakes hit in 1811, millions of acres along the river sank as much as 50 feet, creating even more swampland, which would soon kill the forests. However, the land reclamation efforts went on for more than a hundred years, and by 1930 most of the swamps were gone. Then came the loggers and sawmills, and then the plows. Soon most of the trees were gone, replaced by crops.

The stand of trees in this state park survived the ax and saw. Even though the Great Depression had most of America on its economic knees, local businessmen took up the cause to protect this last stand of timber, and schoolchildren donated pennies, nickels, and dimes to the cause. In 1938 just over 1,000 acres were purchased, and the Big Oak Tree State Park came into being.

Among the towering oak, elm, and hickory trees stand seven trees that are the tallest of their species in Missouri, and two that are the tallest in America. In addition to these trees, the park has green ash, swamp cottonwood, American elm, black willow, persimmon, silver maple, bald cypress, and giant cane. There are also poison ivy and stinging nettles, but you don't have to worry about them because a boardwalk keeps you at a safe distance while keeping your feet dry. The state park information sheet also includes this reassuring sentence: "Although the park has a lot of water snakes, there has never been any verified and documented identification of any venomous snakes such as the cottonmouth (also known as a water moccasin)." That means you can walk along while staring upward with the only danger being that you might sunburn your neck.

Bird-watchers also like the park because 146 species of birds have been counted there, including some that are rare in Missouri, such as the hooded warbler, the Mississippi kite, and the endangered Swainson's warbler.

Ridges and trenches caused by earth movement during the 1811–12 earthquakes in the New Madrid area.

Picnicking is encouraged; the park has one picnic shelter that can be reserved for $30 per day. Other shelters are on a first-come, first-served basis and are free. Two large grills, electricity, and potable water are available. Ten other picnic sites are scattered along the boardwalk and elsewhere in the park. See information at the end of this chapter for telephone numbers and addresses.

To reach New Madrid from the park, go south on MO 102 to the first junction, which will be MO 520. Turn right (or west) and it soon becomes Route WW, which will take you into **New Madrid**, pronounced MAD-rid. This town was the epicenter of the strongest earthquake ever recorded in North America, and perhaps in the world. The immense area covered, and the catastrophic changes the earthquakes brought, have led some seismologists to believe that the New Madrid shocks had a magnitude of XII on the Mercalli intensity scale of I to XII. This scale, which used Roman numerals, was the forefather of the Richter scale (developed in 1938). A XII meant total destruction; the San Francisco earthquake of 1906 was rated only as a VII.

Whatever the exact intensity, and there's no way of knowing, there can be no doubt of its severity; several people lived in the area, and their collective memory of those terrifying days provided a consistent account.

New Madrid was one of the first areas in Missouri to be settled. Two Canadian trappers, Francois and Joseph LeSieur, established a trading post there in 1783 for a St. Louis merchant named Gabriel Cerre. They called the region L'Anse a la Graisse (Cove of Grease) because buffalo and bear, sources of grease, were abundant in the area. In 1789, George Morgan, a veteran of the Revolutionary War, came in, laid out a large city, and called it New Madrid in hopes that the Spanish would look favorably on his undertaking. Morgan didn't stay around long, but the Spanish built a fort and collected duties on the river traffic. By the end of the 18th century, an estimated 600 persons lived in the area. It is not known when the pronunciation changed from Castilian to American English, but pronunciations of towns named for Old World cities had a way of being corrupted, such as Cairo, Illinois, where the Kentucky River enters the Mississippi. That grand Egyptian name is now pronounced like the famous pancake syrup, KAY-ro.

In some accounts of the cataclysmic quake, farm animals and dogs set up a terrible ruckus just before the first quake hit at about 2 AM on December 8, 1811. All accounts by survivors leave no doubt that the earth rose and fell rhythmically like waves in the ocean. People were thrown out of bed onto the floor and were unable to stand on their feet. They crawled out into the darkness and clung to the earth. The earth waves continued until daybreak and throughout that day. This went on day after day. There was no record of anything like it ever happening anywhere in the world before. Gradually, the waves diminished. Then another strong shock came on December 16 and continued all through that day and the next. The shocks continued for several more days, again diminishing in strength; then, on January 23, 1812, another shock hit that residents said was as strong as the first. Still another strong one hit on February 7, which was to be the last big one. It wasn't over, though; almost every day for nearly two years residents felt the earth move, sometimes gently and other times not so gently.

A man in Louisville and another in Ste. Genevieve set out to count all the tremors, but both gave up when they numbered in the hundreds. Researchers have since estimated that more than 1,900 separate tremors, strong enough to be felt 200 miles away, occurred.

The result was catastrophic beyond imagination. The Mississippi was dammed at one point and flowed backward. A waterfall was created upstream from New Madrid, and then it was swept away. The course of the river changed several times, and riverbanks were swept into the current. Trees and parts of houses and barns floated back and forth as the seismic waves created havoc on the river. Islands disappeared and new ones were created. Lakes beside the river were drained and new ones created.

Large areas of the earth sunk up to 15 feet, including the original town of New Madrid. It disappeared forever. Vast fissures were created and then closed, expelling tons of water, sand, and charcoal into the air. Often the air was filled with the stench of sulfur and rotting vegetation. One man told of falling into one of these fissures and seeing occasional flashes of light, apparently from gases being ignited. The sounds of the earthquakes must have been terrifying: the explosions in the fissures, the creaking and groaning of the tortured earth, the roar of the river, the waterfalls being created, the screams of animals.

After several weeks of the continual quakes and chasms opening and closing in the earth, the residents came up with an effective means of avoiding falling into them. The chasms opened in the same direction each time, southwest to northeast, so people felled trees at a right angle to the chasms, northwest to southeast, and at the first hint of a new quake, they climbed onto the trees while the earth sometimes opened beneath them.

The course of the river was changed forever. In Kentucky, Reelfoot Lake was created when the river rushed in to fill one of the many depressions created when the earth dropped. The lake, now part of the Reelfoot National Wildlife Refuge, is currently about 14 miles long, 5 miles wide, and an average of 18-feet deep, which is the depth that this part of the earth fell. Immediately after the earthquakes, the lake was more than 100 miles long.

When the quaking at last stopped, the federal government instituted its first-ever disaster relief fund for survivors. It issued New Madrid certificates, which entitled displaced landowners new acreage in the Louisiana Purchase territory. The Bounty certificates, which were payment in land instead of cash to veterans of the War of 1812, were exchanged for the New Madrid certificates because they offered land elsewhere. This paper chase naturally resulted in speculators who lied and cheated and manipulated the two land grants.

New Madrid was relatively quiet after the earthquakes finally ended, and the surviving townspeople who didn't want to leave stubbornly rebuilt their homes and businesses. They were hampered somewhat by an incredibly annoying group of religious fanatics, who called themselves the Fanatical Pilgrims. Thinking the earthquakes might be a sign from God, they arrived in New Madrid riding on the hope that it was Jerusalem. They were messy people. They were uniformly gaunt, wore rags, and did not believe in bathing. They did not own property, refused to work, and did not bury their dead. Their nourishment of choice was mush and milk served in a communal wooden trough and sucked through hollowed cornstalks. As if these characteristics weren't bad enough, they also burst into private homes, always without warning, while shouting "Praise God" or "Repent."

The earthquakes coincided with the voyages of the great Shawnee chief, Tecumseh, often named as the greatest of the Native American leaders during the European takeover of North America. Tecumseh traveled from tribe to tribe, all across the Midwest and all along the East Coast, from New England to Florida, trying to organize the tribes into a giant army to protect themselves against the white men, who just kept coming and coming, taking more and more land, and shoving the Native Americans aside. He did this for a number of years, beginning around the turn of the 19th century, and during his travels he was often able to mediate local problems within or between tribes, so great were his skills of negotiating and the respect he received. An example is the murdering frenzy the Osage in the New Madrid area got into when they believed that women in their tribe were practicing witchcraft. More than 50 women were found guilty and all were burned to death. When Tecumseh appeared on one of his political visits, so strong was his presence that the fears of witches were forgotten.

His efforts were greatest during 1811–12. His message took on greater urgency and power because his mission coincided with two great natural events: the New Madrid earthquakes and the appearance of a comet, which hovered in the sky above him as he exhorted his people to organize and resist. Apparently, the comet was Halley's comet; it had been reported by astronomers in France in March 1811, and now it hovered over Tecumseh while he was in Missouri. It disappeared when he left.

Similar events happened with other Native American leaders and prophets when the threat of the white man became overpowering. During the last eruption of Glacier Peak in Washington State, between 150 and 200 years ago, a Native American from the Great Lakes region appeared to the Spokan tribe while volcanic ash was falling so thick that it was dark at midday. The prophet warned the tribe of the white people coming, describing the white sails of their ships as wings.

All was reasonably peaceful in the New Madrid area for the next four decades, however during the Civil War, it was the scene of an odd battle. The Confederate forces had been building fortifications along the Mississippi River, and when they lost Forts Donelson and Henry in Kentucky, they moved downstream and set up a stronghold at New Madrid and on No. 10 Island, so named because it was the 10th island downstream from the Ohio. The Union soldiers marched in from Sikeston; the Confederates tried to stop the Union Army's advance by sending out a few men carrying *guidons* to make it look as though they were many. The Union didn't bite, however, and with the Union riders on his heels, the Confederate general barely escaped back to his compound. The heavy bombardment became known as the Battle of Island No. 10. The Union bombardment of the Confederates continued from the night of March 12 through the day and into the night of March 13.

During the night of March 13, the Confederates held a council and realized that their situation was hopeless. When morning came, the Union officers prepared to launch an attack—all their men were at their battle stations waiting for the order. Suddenly two faint forms emerged from the thick fog. They were Confederates carrying white flags. They told the Union soldiers that everyone had left during the night, but that they had slept through the retreat.

New Madrid got a lot of attention, and some frazzled nerves, in 1990 when a persuasive man named Iben Browning said that there was a one-in-two chance that another devastating earthquake would hit the New Madrid area on about December 3, 1990. Browning was a very smart, highly educated man who was trained as a climatologist, not a seismologist. He lived in New Mexico, which struck some people as odd because he was making predictions about a place he had hardly visited. He based his predictions on a peculiar positioning of the moon, which he was certain would upset the earth's gravity and cause another devastating earthquake. Helping his cause was a mild earthquake that struck north of New Madrid. Although most people doubted him, there was enough publicity surrounding his prediction that New Madrid was host to news crews from all over the United States. It was one of those situations in which the news industry was damned if they did send a crew to cover it, and damned if they didn't, because the prediction just might be accurate.

Sue Hubbell, a reporter, was living over in the Missouri Ozarks tending bees and writing what she called a "countrywoman as Erma Bombeck" column for the *St. Louis Post-Dispatch*. She went over to see what the fuss was about. Upon arrival, she counted more than 50 vehicles with news logos and satellite dishes; she wrote in the *New Yorker*, "like Dr. Robertson, who had counted the tremors of 1811–12, I got tired and quit. I looked local, so I was interviewed a lot."

Although many people were understandably nervous about the proceedings, there were enough unusual occurrences during this period to keep people telling stories for years to come. One radio station brought along a 350-pound man and had him jump up and down in a futile attempt to trigger a quake. The Earthquake Awareness Task Force gave out the wrong toll-free number and all calls went to a travel agent in California.

By the end of the long day predicted for the disaster, the biggest nonevent in Missouri history faded, and news crews went back to their newspapers and radio and television stations with nothing more than the news that nothing happened. The man who created the whole thing, Iben Browning, didn't return phone calls that night. Coming to his defense, more or less, the mayor of New Madrid said the town owed Browning their gratitude, because his folly pointed out the need for an emergency response plan for New Madrid.

Today an enormously tall and long levee runs the length of town and protects New Madrid's historic buildings from the Mississippi River. This levee is part of the U.S. Army Corps of Engineers' flood-control system, which involves two long levees. The first is close to the river and protects the farmland and towns against normal flooding. Set back a mile or so is a second levee, which is the second line of defense against the occasional catastrophic flood. In New Madrid, which is right on the river, there is a flood gate to release water trapped by this second levee back into the river.

An observation deck runs 120 feet along the levee and out over the river. It houses an exhibit on the **Civil War Battle of Island No. 10**. Here the Mississippi makes an almost 360-degree turn, bringing part of Kentucky almost into New Madrid's lap.

The town now seems most proud of its several antebellum homes. One of these, the **Hunter-Dawson Home**, is a state historic site and is open for viewing. It was built during 1858 and 1859, using slave labor and craftsmen from St. Louis, and it has been restored to its original appearance. It also has one of the nation's best collections of Mitchell and Rammelsberg furniture, which was the premier furniture maker of the 19th century. Another is the **Bloomfield Home**, more than 150 years old and the oldest brick home in the area. Yet another of these mansions, known as the **A. B. Hunter Sr. Mansion**, now houses the New Madrid County Health Center.

The **New Madrid Historical Museum** is in a former saloon on Main Street and has displays related to all major events in the town's history, including numerous items from and depictions of the 1811–12 earthquakes, the town's unusual role in the Civil War, and the grim history of the local Native Americans.

IN THE AREA

Lodging and dining are very limited in this small town. Because it is near Sikeston, most visitors go there. Other attractions in the area are listed here.

Hunter-Dawson State Historic Site, Dawson Road near First Street, New Madrid. Call 573-748-5340. Open daily. Admission charged. Web site: www.mostateparks.com/hunterdawson.htm.

New Madrid Historical Museum, 1 Main Street, New Madrid. Call 573-748-5944. Open daily. Admission charged. Web site: www.newmadridmuseum.com.

Towosahgy State Historic Site and Big Oak Tree State Park,
13640 S. Highway, East Prairie. Call 573-649-3149, or 573-748-5340
to reserve picnic sites. Web site: www.mostateparks.com/
towosahgy.htm.

Poplar Bluff to Branson

Estimated length: 200 miles
Estimated time: one, perhaps two days

Getting there: From Poplar Bluff in southeast Missouri, take US 160 west nearly all the way across the state to Branson. The winding, two-lane route can be used as a baseline from which to begin several trips northward toward the Missouri River and St. Louis. Also, you will probably want to make short side trips off this artery to see rivers, enormous springs, gristmills, canyons, and creeks.

Highlights: Ozark **springs**, swift rivers, crafts, **gristmills**, man-made lakes, and **Shepherd of the Hills country**.

US 160 twists and turns its way through the heart of the **Missouri Ozarks,** touching on the best the region has to offer. It begins near Poplar Bluff and ends about 200 miles later in Springfield, after turning sharply north near Branson to leave the Ozark Mountains for the plateau country around Springfield. This route has become more and more popular with people driving to and from Branson, where country-and-western stars, and pop musicians on the downhill slope of their fame, have built their own theaters.

Old cabin in the Missouri Ozarks

Poplar Bluff is on the line of demarcation between the swampland of eastern Missouri and the Ozark Highlands. For a long time, the swampland was both coveted and feared by entrepreneurs. The Mississippi valley south of St. Louis was one of the unhealthiest places on earth. The standing water of the swamps not only harbored poisonous snakes and other dangerous beasts, but also harbored clouds of disease-bearing mosquitoes, sand flies, and other insects. Malaria and black fever were common. The reason the vast majority of people gave for taking to the Oregon Trail in the 19th-century migration to the West Coast was that the Oregon Country was healthy. This was also a major reason people gave up rich farmland in river bottomlands for the rocky, thin soil of the Ozark Highlands. It was much healthier in the hills, away from the standing water and clouds of insects which, some old timers said, could kill a horse by plugging its nostrils.

Poplar Bluff was built on the banks of the Black River and named for a grove of yellow poplar trees growing along one bank of the river. It was a notoriously unhealthy place to live until the swampland on the eastern side of the river was drained. The town was also leveled during the Civil War by the renegades who roamed the Border States, murdering and robbing for recreation more than from political conviction.

Today Poplar Bluff is a commercial center of about 20,000 inhabitants, with all services for travelers.

US 160 starts south of Poplar Bluff at an intersection where MO 67 turns due south to Arkansas. US 160 heads due west toward **Doniphan**, where the beautiful MO 21 heads northward toward St. Louis, a route that is described in Chapter 8 of this book. The highway curves around the northern edge of Doniphan and goes directly into the rugged Ozark hills and hollows. It is not a fast highway and you should not be in a hurry. You might not only miss the scenery, you might also miss one of the many curves.

This portion of the drive is through the **Mark Twain National Forest** which, in this area, is famous for springs. Geologists measure springs in terms of magnitude, with first-magnitude springs producing at least 65 million gallons of water daily. The **Ozark National Scenic Riverways**, beginning in the Doniphan area and following the Current and Jacks Fork Rivers northward, has more first-magnitude springs than any other place in the world. Missouri springs that meet this criterion include: **Big Spring** (286 million gallons), **Alley Spring** (81 million gallons), **Blue Spring** (93 million gallons), **Round Spring** (33 million gallons), and **Welch Spring** (75 million gallons). One of the most popular springs in this area is also one of the smallest to have a name. **Falling Spring** flows out of a bluff, making a modest waterfall, as shown in the cover image for this book. **Falling Spring Mill** is at the base of the bluff, looking as though the builder some 80 years ago had paintings and photographs in mind. The site is often used for weddings and other occasions. To reach the spring, go 12 miles north of Alton on MO 19 and watch for the sign pointing to the spring. It is at the end of a 3-mile-long gravel road.

In an article written for the National Park Service, Mike Gossett said that each spring has its own unique sound, "ranging from a loud roar to a soft splashing." He said that all springs are dissolving the walls of their underground routes through the limestone, and that, in the case of Big Spring, the daily load of calcium carbonate hauled away by the spring is in the neighborhood of 175 tons—per day. If this is true, it is little wonder that some of these underground rivers eventually collapse, as did the stream near Thayer in the Grand Gulf, described in Chapter 9.

Alton is next on the way west, a town of fewer than 1,000 people that is the seat of Oregon County. Records of the county are complete because they were hidden in a cave overlooking Piney Creek, to prevent the marauders from destroying them. Fire was the weapon of choice for the bushwhackers who roamed the hills, destroying buildings, towns, and lives for sport. Alton's records remained in the cave from 1862 until 1865, and during that terrible period the courthouse indeed did burn, with a little help from bad people.

MO 19, described in Chapter 9, crosses US 160 in Alton.

The countryside opens up and flattens out a bit until you reach **West Plains**. The town earned that name because it was founded at a spring in the treeless area west of **Thomasville**, the town founded some years earlier on the Eleven Point River. The first known settler in West Plains was a hunter who lived near the spring during the summer months. In 1839 he sold his cabin and whatever else he had built to a man from Tennessee named Josiah Howell, who was a town builder, and whose efforts were memorialized when Howell County was formed. When the Civil War broke out, West Plains was abandoned to the aforementioned guerrillas who came through, more interested in terrorizing people and burning houses and barns than striking blows for political philosophies. The war itself was horrible enough, but the general meanness it unleashed among the poor hill people was an even darker story. One band, led by a man named Watson, burned the abandoned homes of West Plains to the ground. When a former citizen returned, the only living thing he found was a cat.

The town was rebuilt around the spring, and when a railroad was built through town in 1883, West Plains's future was assured. Over the next century, it grew to become a trading center for a large section of Missouri and northern Arkansas. The post office was built over the spring, and later the building was turned into the public library. Before the library outgrew the old post office building and was moved several blocks away, you could ask a librarian to see the spring and she would oblige. Today the building is owned by the Baptist Church and is used for classes. The spring still gurgles happily, and you can still go downstairs to see it.

As US 160 continues its tour beyond West Plains, it runs through countryside typical of the Ozarks today—no row crops, only open fields for grazing and growing hay. The Ozarks, once so poor and littered with rough shacks, has so many modern homes now that it looks like a suburb with exceptionally wide spacing. Unlike northern Missouri where people gave up living out in the country and moved to town, most people in the Ozarks work in town and keep the farms for the love of living on them and to have something to do. The economy in the Ozarks is thriving because of tourism and as a place for retirees to buy inexpensive land.

It was not always like this, of course. Until long after World War II, people still tried to work this land and many spirits were broken in the process. It was impossible to raise cash crops because the poor soil would only grow enough for subsistence farming. The crops included corn and wheat, which were ground into flour and meal and used for the families and animals. Other crops were for silage and hay. Women had large gardens and canned everything they grew. Fruit and nut trees completed the menu.

A scene the author witnessed in the 1950s tells the story of working the land in the Ozarks very well. A man was plowing a field with a single horse pulling the plow. He was standing with the reins tied, one looped over his right shoulder and the other beneath his left arm. It was obviously hot and almost certainly humid because his shirt was stained with sweat. He stood with his head thrown back as if trying to catch a breeze to dry the sweat on his neck. The horse stood, head down in fatigue. It was not difficult to imagine how hard the work was because the land was littered with rocks of all sizes and there were roots from the trees that were competing with each other in the meager soil. Each rock, each root would snag the plow, jerking at the man's arms and shoulders, and causing the harness to jerk on the hames and rub the horse's hide. This is what the man and horse would have been doing day after day, year after year until they wore out completely. You could smell the earth and sweat of the horse and man, feel the difficulty of walking with one foot in the soft dirt and the other on firm ground, and the incredibly hard work of holding the plow at the proper angle while geeing and hawing the horse to keep a straight line. Compound this with the extreme heat and it would have been truly miserable; the man's shirt, made of a flour sack, got so hot in the sun that it would have burned him when the over- all straps pressed the hot cotton against his shoulders and back.

If you know the Ozarks of that period you would know that down at one end of the field the man had buried a gallon water jug, and that the jug would be wrapped in wet burlap so the evaporation would keep the water cool, and you would know how the water that came from a spring or a well out of the limestone smelled and tasted, and you would remember the soft, bass thunking sound the corn cob stop- per made when you pulled it from the jug. And you would also know how the horse smelled and sounded, and you could hear the harness creaking and the trace chains clattering, and when the day was over and the horse was unharnessed, he would shake himself several times, then roll on the ground.

The highway twists and winds across the countryside and passes towns that appear on the maps but consist of just one building, or sometimes there is just a crossroads with a bare spot where a building once stood. About 40 miles west of West Plains, the road suddenly drops down a steep hill to a place named **Tecumseh**, which is just above a bridge that crosses the narrow neck of the upper end of Norfork Lake. The lake is a result of the first of several dams built in Arkansas between Tecumseh and Branson, beginning in the 1940s, to bring electricity to this part of the country. This part of the Ozarks is partially flooded with man-made lakes: **Norfork, Bull Shoals, Taneycomo, Table Rock**. All except Taneycomo are the result of hydroelectric dams built across the border in Arkansas, and all have had more of a positive than negative effect, because the land they covered was seldom good for farming and the vast lakes created a tourist industry. When Norfork Dam was built south of Mountain Home, Arkansas, during World War II, it created a lot of jobs for boys too young to go off to war and for men who were too old to fight.

While the dams brought hard-labor jobs to the hills, the resulting lakes brought the tourism that helped change the use of Ozark lands. The first jobs created were for woodsmen to fell trees and remove stumps, to prepare for the waters that would flood the river valley for miles and miles. Men who for years had not earned wages now were on a payroll, bringing home the same amount of money each week, and learning about payroll deductions for Social Security and the Internal Revenue Service. This experience prepared many for work in the defense industry in World War II.

Guy Howard, the "Walkin' Preacher of the Ozarks" often came through this area on his sojourns, and one stop was always at the one-room schoolhouse at **Hog Danger**, which is a few miles east of the Norfork River. Hog Danger got its name many years ago because hogs liked to crawl beneath the schoolhouse and they made a terrible racket down there, snorting and squealing and carrying on. The schoolteacher could hardly teach under these conditions, so he heated water on the woodstove, then poured it through cracks in the floor to flush out the hogs. Thus, *hog danger.*

The Ozark Mountains were cleared of deer and bear by people who were hunting for food for their tables and who ignored the game laws. In most cases, they needed the food. As life became easier and people could afford to buy red meat, the fish and game departments were able to make headway on reintroducing native animals. Today Missouri has thousands of deer, and the wild turkey population has increased dramatically. It is such a friendly place for game that even armadillos have begun migrating north from Texas, adding variety in species and numbers to the road kill statistics.

Just before you reach Tecumseh you will see Route PP heading north. This is the beginning of the gristmill loop described in Chapter 7.

A short distance west of Tecumseh is Route J, which leads 2 miles south to **Howards Ridge**, named for a man who ran a mail route on a saddle horse and eventually established a permanent post office. First you pass the **Faye Cemetery**, where Jack Satterfield is buried; his headstone reveals that he was killed for his money and that he is "Gone but not forgotten." Apparently everyone in the community knew who the two murderers were but nobody would cooperate with the legal system. No arrests were made and the deathbed confessions some expected never came.

The **Howards Ridge Cemetery** is a showplace for the community, and in fact is probably the only organization bearing the community's name. The little church across the road from the cemetery was built in the late 1930s and has hardly changed, except that electricity has been added to replace the hissing gas lanterns.

The cemetery is much the same as any other country cemetery, except that off to one side, some distance from the neat rows of graves and modest headstones, is the grave of Roscoe Jackson. "Red" Jackson, so known because of his hair color, was born just south of Howards Ridge in 1901 and died on May 21, 1937. Cause of death was hanging; he was the last person executed by hanging in Missouri.

Jackson was in and out of trouble most of his life. His first legal problem came in his teens, when he was arrested for carrying a pistol that he threatened to use on another boy who was pursuing the same girl. He was arrested for carrying a concealed weapon, tried, found guilty, and sentenced to the state penitentiary. Jackson was paroled, but he jumped parole and went to Oklahoma. He was brought back and his attorney was able to convince the court he should not go to prison, but before the attorney could tell Jackson, he and another prisoner threw kerosene on the sheriff's dog and set it on fire. He was sent back to the penitentiary and remained there for some time.

This became a pattern with Jackson. Each time he was released, his next crimes were worse. Each time he was arrested, he escaped. And he kept killing people who offered him rides while he was on the run. Finally, in 1934, he went to trial in Galena, in Stone County, and was convicted and sentenced to death by hanging. People came from miles around, some with small children, to watch the hanging. On the eve of his death, Jackson confessed to three other unsolved murders. He stood on the trap door of the gallows built for the occasion, said "So

Church across from Howards Ridge Community Cemetery

long, boys," and was hanged. His body was brought back to Howards Ridge for burial. The local cemetery board has resisted efforts of some ghoulish folks who want to erect a sign telling Red Jackson's gloomy story.

Soon after Jackson's hanging, the Missouri legislature passed a statute changing the form of execution to the gas chamber.

The one-room schoolhouse is long gone. When schools were consolidated, the little building was torn down to make way for a new road; the workmen found that saplings had been used for rafters and the bark was still on them. This schoolhouse was the community center and community church until the little church was built across the road from the cemetery. Sometimes an itinerant preacher would come through to scare the folks into putting money in the hat he passed around while the congregation sang sad songs. Sometimes a local celebrity, such as Slim Pickins Wilson of KWTO in Springfield, would give a concert.

Other performers came through who did not preach or sing. One man in particular, who is still discussed, gave a performance that included feats of strength, such as having a tug-of-war with several men and holding his own. His major stunt was breaking several bottles and jars in a wooden box, then taking off his shoes and jumping into the box. It was a frightening thing for children, and apparently the jumper as well, because witnesses said he sat perched on the teacher's desk a long time while the gas lanterns hissed before finally launching himself into the broken glass. He didn't suffer a single cut.

Gainesville is one of those towns of fewer than 1,000 people that hardly changes from decade to decade. The courthouse has always been the dominant building and probably always will be. It is one of those county seats where you can go into almost any office and be treated like a friendly neighbor, and somebody in the courthouse will have an answer to nearly any question.

The countryside from West Plains to Gainesville and onward to the Branson area consists of oak timber mixed with ash, hickory, and an occasional dogwood and persimmon, and always with thick underbrush. In this brush you will find blackberries, wild strawberries, wild grapes, and also poison ivy and poison oak. On that underbrush you will also find chiggers and ticks, and you must also watch for snakes because the Ozarks hosts several kinds, including the poisonous copperheads that blend in with the leaves.

It is about 60 miles from Gainesville to **Branson**, and according to one economic report a few years ago, this east–west strip along the Arkansas border is expected to grow rapidly, thanks in part to the interest Branson has brought to the Ozarks.

There is a tendency toward gentrification of the Ozarks as more money is brought in. More and more large cattle operations have come in to let the cattle graze on the open country created by the farmers who struggled to raise crops on the poor soil during the warm months. During the winter, the fields are turned into feedlots, with hay served to these cattle daily.

US 160 becomes more beautiful the farther west you drive. Steep hills have panoramic views of the timbered hills, and you'll find several lovely spots along the shores of Bull Shoals Lake near **Sundown, Theodosia,** and **Ocie.** Just beyond is the beginning of the **Shepherd**

of the Hills area, named for a famous novel with that title written by Harold Bell Wright and published in 1907.

In a sense, the novel created this part of Missouri, much as Mark Twain created Hannibal. The novel was made into a silent film and later into a successful talkie. For most of this century, people have gone to Shepherd of the Hills country to see **Inspiration Point**, the **Shepherd of the Hills Homestead**, and other places Wright wrote about. The novel is deeply religious in tone—Wright was an ordained minister and preached at many churches throughout the area—and this story of a minister and the backward, superstitious people he tried to shepherd into the ways of Christianity became an immediate success. Many of Wright's fans have visited this area, and souvenir hunters stripped a house that was featured in the book.

Another universally loved writer, Vance Randolph, wrote only about the Ozarks, and lived there most of his adult life. Randolph was a folklorist, and he recorded stories, music, and the way people spoke. In spite of the implied superiority that folklorists, anthropologists, and other researchers carry with them, Randolph seems to have won the complete trust of the Ozark people he studied, and he convinced them that his interest in them was a compliment. He lived variously in Galena and Pineville, Missouri, and also across the border in Arkansas at Eureka Springs and Fayetteville. He was to Ozarks folklore what Alan Lomax was to Appalachia.

Randolph's approach was to first be accepted as a friend: when he won someone's trust, he never betrayed it. According to Ozarks folklore, he wrote that "I listened to story-tellers in taverns and village stores, on the courthouse steps, at the mill while our corn was a-grinding, beneath the arbors where backwoods Christians congregate. Several of my best pieces were recorded in a house of mourning, when we sat up all night to keep cats away from the corpse." This latter duty was necessary because of a local superstition that, if a cat even sniffed a corpse, horrible things would happen to the survivors.

Randolph wrote many collections of stories and took photographs of many people, which, a decade after his death in 1980, have been recognized as other important contributions. One of the funniest collections was published after his death. It was a set of raunchy stories that couldn't be included in his books for the schools and public libraries. Good taste prevents printing the name of the book here, but it involves something that little boys—and some men—love to do in the snow.

Like so much of pioneer America, the Ozarks had its share of violence, especially during the Reconstruction years following the Civil War, when the country was licking its wounds. In the Branson area, the Bald Knobbers, a vigilante group, held its meetings on a hilltop with no vegetation, so they could see anyone coming. The group was immediately popular, and in 1885 they broke into the Taney County jail and lynched two brothers being held for shooting a storekeeper. They called on drunks to scare them into the ways of righteousness, they beat men who were living in sin with women, and they beat known adulterers.

The group remained a force for two to three years, committing some murders and to a large degree controlling Taney County. Eventually, the Bald Knobbers faded away—some members went to jail, others were killed, and plain fatigue set in. Similar bands of self-righteous vigilantes popped up in other communities throughout the Ozarks, and in many cases, the leaders were guilty of the crimes against the sanctity of marriage they sought to punish. Whether this was an attempt to throw gossipers off the scent, or to repay society for their own sins by punishing others, is a question best left to psychologists and other students of human foibles.

The tourist industry in the area around Lake Taneycomo and Branson was born with Wright's *Shepherd of the Hills*, and it has grown steadily over the years. **Silver Dollar City**, an Ozarks theme park, became a success, and a local musical group called the Bald Knobbers—of course—built a theater for its performances after the auditorium the band used in the city hall became too small. This was the start of the country-music explosion in Branson. The Presley family came next and built a theater for themselves, then the Foggy River Boys, then the Plummer family, then the Bob-O-Links.

Boxcar Willie was the first big-name performer to have a theater. He was followed by the Sons of the Pioneers, Mel Tillis, Ray Stevens, Johnny and June Carter Cash, Andy Williams, and Willie Nelson, among many others.

The best definition of the Branson success came from one singer who said he would much rather the fans come to him at one place than go on the road throughout most of the year, taking himself to the fans.

IN THE AREA

You won't find many places to sleep other than the standard motels unless you venture off the main highway onto MO 19 or MO 21. Bed-and-breakfasts hardly exist along this route. Poplar Bluff, Doniphan, West Plains, and Gainesville all have standard motels. Food is available all along the route, but don't expect much beyond highway food.

OTHER CONTACTS

Bull Shoals Lake and White River Area Chamber of Commerce, Theodosia. Call 417-273-4362.

Doniphan/Ripley County Chamber of Commerce, Doniphan. Call 573-996-2212. Web site: www.ripleycountymissouri.org.

Gainesville Chamber of Commerce, Gainesville. Call 417-679-4913.

Greater West Plains Area Chamber of Commerce, West Plains. Call 417-256-4433. Web site: www.wpchamber.com.

The Walkin' Preacher of the Ozarks

In 1944 the world was war weary. World War II had been going on for five years in Europe and Asia, and for three years for the United States. But the end seemed to be in sight. In the U.S., the prosperity brought by the war to the middle class and the poor was being taken for granted by now, because every available man could find work and women were doing work normally reserved for men.

The war had forced people in the Ozark hills out into the world, either to fight or to take jobs in the defense industry. Women had followed their husbands to ports or other points of embarkation, and many stayed there to work and wait. As a result, hill people were seeing what the rest of American society was like, and an emotional and spiritual tug-of-war started between the old ways and the ways of everyone else. Fire-and-brimstone preachers put up the last line of defense in an effort to save the old-time religious ways, but their work was becoming more and more difficult.

One preacher who was up for the challenge was Guy Howard, an Iowa farm boy who was born into a Quaker family and who developed a more rigorous attitude toward religion; eventually he decided to become an itinerant preacher, so he began walking south. He walked through Iowa and down through the rich farmland north of the Missouri River, and on southward into the Ozark Mountains. In Iowa he found his calling. In the Ozark Mountains he found his home.

He walked from shack to shack, from schoolhouse to schoolhouse, from town to town, always walking and always preaching. If he couldn't find a building to use for his revivals, he built brush arbors. A framework was built of saplings and then covered with leafy branches, making a surprisingly waterproof gathering place. His message was more gentle than that of most preachers. He did not shout. He did not incite the congregations into glossallia or extreme displays of public emotion. Nor did he compare denominations with one another. Instead, he believed that all denominations were treated equally by God. He preached forgiveness. He did not demand money from his congregations; it was not unusual for these preachers to threaten heavenly retribution on those who did not put at least a dollar in the collection plate. Howard was different.

"You shorely must be aworkin' fer the Lord fer ye hain't beggin' fer money not atalkin' denomination," someone told him, according to the autobiography he wrote.

Howard carried very little with him on his constant journey: a change of clothing, always his Bible, and sometimes another book or two. He relied on the generosity of the poor hill folk for meals and a place to sleep, and what little money he had was given to him either from taking up a collection at the end of each sermon or from meeting people on the road who would hand him a dollar, sometimes as much as $10, when they parted company. His income was about $14 a month.

He kept walking. At the end of the first year, he computed his mileage and found that he had walked more than 4,000 miles. He stopped sometimes to spend a few months in an area, and sometimes he talked the community into building a church of its own. Sometimes he took on the job of teaching all eight grades in a schoolhouse. But basically, for more than a decade, he walked from place to place, and then back again.

By the early 1940s he was married and had two children. When his wife became seriously ill, Howard had no choice but to take her to

Barnes Hospital in St. Louis for treatment. He never said where the money came from to pay the hospital, so the general assumption is that she was treated for free as a charity patient.

Howard knew his wife would be gone several weeks and then would need several months to recuperate. So he placed their two young daughters in an orphanage and went off to continue preaching, feeling guilty and inadequate. His wife eventually recovered enough to leave the hospital, so he celebrated this event by taking her on a walking and hitchhiking trip from St. Louis to Springfield, down into Arkansas, and across the Ozark Mountains to Mountain Home, and then back to Gainesville. There he met perhaps his most important benefactor, John Harlin, a religious banker who was somewhat of a benevolent dictator of Ozark County. Harlin talked Howard into staying in Gainesville at least for a while, and helped him buy the first house Howard ever owned.

All the while Howard kept preaching. He became a moral crusader by setting up sting operations to close rowdy bars. For a while, he was a Boy Scout leader, and with the cooperation of parents, he used the boys in sting operations; he'd get them to buy beer in roadhouses, with the sheriff or police chief waiting outside. He wasn't able to make a dent in one tavern's business, so he took to going in every afternoon, ordering a cup of coffee, and sitting for half an hour sipping his coffee. He knew his presence would put a damper on the roughnecks' fun, but it always resumed when he left.

Then, in 1944, he became a national celebrity. He was interviewed on local and national radio shows fairly often; the chairman of a book publishing company, Harper & Brothers, heard him telling of his experiences with the Ozark hill folks, and immediately got in touch with him. Howard wrote a memoir about his life, *The Walkin' Preacher of the Ozarks*. It was a best seller.

With this success came resentment and charges of betrayal, and Howard found himself less than popular with the people of whom he wrote. He told the story of an elderly blind woman who had given birth to 11 children—and that her husband was also her father.

He wrote about children who died of poisoned moonshine, and repeated their deathbed statements. He told about all sorts of evil acts and superstitions. Anything that went on in the Ozarks was raw material for his book.

Although Howard did not reveal the names of the guilty, he had committed the unpardonable crime of talking about the hill folk to outsiders. Threats were made against him and his family.

Howard may have been naive to the point of being irresponsible in his work and the effect it had on his family, but he was not a coward. He faced his enemies and refused to leave the Ozarks. Still, his credibility was compromised and he was never completely accepted again by the community. He continued writing, and switched over to fiction, only weakly disguising his subjects' identities.

Howard's success bred satire, and in 1951 a song called "Missouri Walking Preacher" appeared on jukeboxes and was played on the radio.

Ol' Doc Bible was a hard rock reliable
preacher in old Mizzou;
When he got lyrical,
Many was the miracle
Doc was liable to do.

Howard was incensed. He sued RCA Victor, Decca, and Capitol record companies in federal court for $1 million, stating that the song was a "burlesque on me and maligns my work and Christianity." He added, "The boogie-woogie, beer-hall music of this song has brought me much grief and caused friends to question my faith and integrity."

Two of the three companies paid Howard about $4,000 each. Capitol continued fighting Howard, but newspapers of the period didn't bother reporting on the outcome. This battle was one of the last mentions of Howard in newspapers and magazines. He drifted into obscurity and is seldom mentioned, even in the Ozarks where he was such a major figure in the 1940s and 1950s.

No doubt his intentions were pure because he worked so hard for many years, often at the risk of his and his family's well-being. He would be unconcerned about his current obscurity because he never actually sought personal attention. But in putting his memoirs to paper, Howard lost his usually good judgment and told many, many secrets that had been entrusted to him. He was never completely trusted again by those he had tried to help.

The Gristmill Loop

Estimated length: 60 miles
Estimated time: half day

Getting there: Go west on US 160 from West Plains approximately 30 miles to Route PP, just east of the village of Tecumseh. If you come to a bridge across the Norfork Lake, you have gone too far. Go north on Route PP and watch for Route PP318 and the signs to Dawt Mill, which is about a mile off Route PP and down a steep hill to the left (west). From Dawt Mill, return to Route PP, which becomes Route H after an intersection with MO 14. Continue north on Route H to Hodgson Mill, which is less than 50 feet off the road on the right. Continue north to the intersection of Route H and MO 181. Turn left (south) on MO 181; Zanoni Mill is near the intersection of MO 181 and Route N. To reach Rockbridge, take Route N north from Zanoni. Rockbridge is just north of the intersection of Route N and MO 95. The driving instructions are not as confusing as they sound, but you should have a detailed map showing all smaller roads. Free maps and brochures are available from the Chamber of Commerce in West Plains and Gainesville, and you can also find maps on the Internet.

Hodgson Mill

Highlights: This relatively short drive will give you access to four grist-mills in various conditions. The first one, **Dawt Mill**, shows more clearly than the others how mills and dams were built before electricity came to the area. The second on the loop is perhaps the most photographed historical site in Missouri, **Hodgson Mill**. The third, **Zanoni Mill**, is now mostly a decoration for a beautiful country inn; and the fourth, **Rockbridge**, is the centerpiece of a popular resort. Spending a day visiting these mills is a pleasant way to see some of the out-of-the-way places in the Ozarks and to talk to the people who own or operate the mills today. None, by the way, is still in commercial operation and only one still functions, but all can be visited.

Those who grew up in the Ozarks before World War II will have memories of these mills: It was a lucky day when children could go with their fathers to the mill with a load of corn or wheat to be ground, because it meant a day without fieldwork, a chance to visit with other kids and to hear the machinery creaking and groaning, and to watch the big wheel being turned by the rushing water.

Of course, getting to the mill in a horse-drawn wagon was usually an uncomfortable experience. Most "iron-tired wagons" didn't have a hint of a suspension system, just the wooden wheels with iron or steel hoops. Sometimes the seat would have rudimentary springs, but not always, and passengers often preferred standing behind the seat and holding it for balance, letting their knees absorb the shocks. Those who owned wagons built from old cars and trucks usually had rubber tires, and it was the difference between riding in misery and riding in luxury.

Visiting these mills today will give you an idea of how isolated many people were in the Ozarks until World War II, and even after that; yet it's surprising how well the mills functioned. They represented a substantial investment by the owners, because all machinery had to be purchased elsewhere and shipped to the site. Sometimes the stone burrs, which ground the wheat, barley, corn, and oats, had to be imported all the way from Europe. It has been said that the best burrs came from France.

Very little money changed hands between the miller and the farmers. The miller charged a toll, from 10 to 20 percent of the grain, which was weighed before it was milled.

Dawt Mill (or Old Dawt Mill as it was already called 50 years ago) is 2 miles north of US 160 on a high bank over the North Fork of the White River, where the river still runs free. The low dam still stands. This mill is the only one that still functions, and it offers demonstrations of milling cornmeal, flour, and feed, as well as blacksmithing and other country crafts. The store sells food and gifts. It is a beautiful spot for a picnic. The mill is also used as a conference center for business and club meetings and retreats.

Four choices of lodging—five if you include a fee campground—are available at the Dawt Mill. The **Cotton Gin Inn** has eight two-room suites. The **Dinnel Log Cabin** looks rustic but is air-conditioned and equipped with a complete kitchen and country furniture. The **Hodgson House** has four units, or suites, and the **Cabin-in-the-Woods** can sleep up to six people. Dining is available in the **Chuck Wagon Restaurant**, and you can stock your room or suite with food from the deli and bakery. Visit the Dawt Mill Web site listed at the end of this chapter for more information about these accomodations.

Hodgson Mill is the most photographed mill in the state, and as such is the best known of the four. It was used in Salem cigarette commercials, and the late Euell Gibbons used it as a backdrop for his cereal commercials.

Although it is now called Hodgson Mill, for a long time the mill was a partnership between the Aid and Hodgson families, and most old-timers still call it by that double name, Aid-Hodgson. The schoolhouse-red building is very picturesque, with old trees framing it and a small waterfall in front that seems to insist that you take photographs. A tip to photographers: The afternoon sun lights the front of the building and the waterfall, and autumn is the best time for photos because of the colors. In summer the leaves are so thick that you can hardly see through them to the mill.

The mill was built in 1861, and rebuilt in 1897, against a steep hillside and over a spring that produces nearly 29 million gallons of water daily that flows into the Bryant River. The building was a popular community center and often used for neighborhood dances because the cool spring water (a constant 58 degrees) kept the building cool enough for strenuous dancing, without excessive perspiration.

In addition to powering the mill, the spring was used to power a cotton gin, a lumber mill, a clothing factory, and an electricity-generating plant in the days before the Rural Electrification Agency brought power lines into the Ozarks.

A mill in Gainesville currently has rights to the Hodgson Mill name, and uses it on its flour, which is ground in a modern plant. At the time of this writing, Hodgson Mill was going through an ownership change and plans for the future were not complete.

The **Rockbridge gristmill** on Spring Creek is probably the oldest of the group. Nobody is quite certain when the first mill was built on this site, only that it predated the Civil War. After the first mill was built, the town of Rockbridge grew around it, and for a while it was the seat of Ozark County. The little town had a bank, a general store, and a church, along with several homes, but its remote location was its undoing. Gainesville was much more accessible and in the center of an area of population growth, so it took over as the county seat; Rockbridge declined to the point that the gristmill was the only viable business remaining.

Zanoni Mill

The town buildings and mill were in a state of disrepair until Lile and Edith Amyx bought the whole works in 1954, and began restoring the site. They stocked the millpond with rainbow trout, and for the past several years Rockbridge has been a popular resort complex called the **Rainbow Trout & Game Ranch**. The owners keep Spring Creek stocked with rainbow trout for guests. Cabins have been added near the general store, which also houses a good restaurant, gift shop, and cafe.

Zanoni Mill was built on Pine Creek about the time of the Civil War, and at one time shared the creek with a water-powered sawmill. The mill was a social center; one owner used the upper floor as a dance hall until the mill burned in 1905. Another mill was built on the site, and it continued operating until 1951. Not much is left of the mill today. It is part of a complex, known as the **Zanoni Mill Ranch**, on a man-made lake that includes a large colonial home with guest rooms and a separate hotel. Social functions, such as weddings, are a staple of this resort.

IN THE AREA

Dawt Mill, Tecumseh. Call 888-884-3298 or 417-284-3540. Web site: www.dawtmill.com.

Hodgson Mill, Tecumseh. Call 417-261-2556. The mill is open from mid-May through mid-October and has a gift shop that sells locally-made crafts.

Rockbridge Rainbow Trout & Game Ranch, Rockbridge. Call 417-679-3619. Web site: www.rockbridgemo.com.

Zanoni Mill Ranch, Zanoni. Call 417-679-2181. Web site: www.zanonimillinn.com.

CHAPTER

8

Doniphan to St. Louis

Estimated length: 150 miles
Estimated time: one day

Getting there: From Doniphan, head north on MO 21 through the Saint Francois Mountains and the mining district.

Highlights: You will go past some of Missouri's best **state parks**, many **springs**, and an assortment of small, picturesque towns.

Some highways seem to exist primarily for the sheer joy of driving them in the spring and fall, preferably in a sports car or, at the very least, a convertible, manual transmission optional, but preferred. If you are fortunate enough to be with the one you love, or on the way to see her or him, so much the better.

MO 21 is a good example of an extremely drivable road. It presents a mild challenge because it is crooked and hilly, but it has curves rather than corners and gentle rises rather than steep hills. Wooden fences line it, giant hardwood trees form a canopy in places, and early and late in the day the sun flickers hypnotically through the leaves. It is a highway for the mobile show-off as well as for those who love

Elephant Rocks State Park

the challenge of driving on a road that can be a joy, a frightening experience. It all depends on how you drive it. During the warmer three seasons, you will often share it with motorcyclists out for a thrill.

This is broken country, with steep but low hills, outcroppings of rocks, and lots of timber. MO 21 is a popular route for *St. Louis Post-Dispatch* photographers, who come out in October to photograph the autumn foliage. Occasionally, as with other lovely highways in Missouri, you will come to a stretch of highway with trees from each side touching each other as they form a canopy overhead. If you are here in the autumn, go for a walk in the woods just to listen to the sound of the dry leaves. Walking on autumn leaves is as noisy as walking on potato chips. There's no sneaking up on unsuspecting wildlife in these conditions.

Going from south to north, MO 21 begins as AR 115 in Arkansas, but when it crosses into Missouri, the number loses 94 digits, and meanders northward, looking like a route that would be drawn by a small boy. It goes fairly straight for a while, then suddenly darts left or right several miles, resumes its northeast direction, gets bored, and zigs and zags a few times more until it reaches its final destination of the St. Louis suburb of Afton, where it butts into MO 30. On the north side of MO 30, it becomes Rock Hill Road. Your beautiful and exciting drive on MO 21 is now a memory.

Before that happens, you will have driven by the **Ozark National Scenic Riverways**, through Missouri's premier **iron-mining district**, and past the highest point in the state and the spectacular state parks near this point.

You will begin the drive by turning north off the cross-state US 160 onto MO 21. If you follow only the highways, you won't see much of **Doniphan**, and it is worth at least a drive through to see the 19th-century architecture and the **Current River Heritage Museum**, on the downtown square. The museum contains memorabilia from the Civil War and the logging industry. It has a one-room schoolhouse and a genealogical library.

MO 21 joins US 60 just west of **Ellsinore** for a few miles, then leaves it and continues on its own without entering **Van Buren**. If you are in the area at mealtime, or nearing the end of the day, Van Buren is only about 10 miles out of your way and is one of the main towns along the Ozark National Scenic Riverways. In fact, it is the last major town on the Current River at the southern end of the designated riverways and, as such, Van Buren is one of the major resort areas along the Current River. About 3 miles south of town is the appropriately named **Big Spring**, probably the largest spring in the nation. It bursts forth from the ground with great force and forms a stream that averages 276 million gallons daily; after a short run, it empties into the Current River.

In general, Van Buren's main reason for existence is the river and its main business is selling float trips and renting flotation devices, ranging from inner tubes to canoes and several variations in between. While tourism is the major industry in Van Buren today, at one time it was a major timber town with an abundance of hardwoods to feed the sawmills. Most of the timber you'll see now is second growth.

In this area you will find a half a dozen places to stay, ranging from a National Park Service campground to an RV park to motels. Restaurants tend more toward country cafés, unpretentious and friendly. You will also find two modest museums that show some of the area's history.

Back on MO 21, you will continue the pleasant drive along the crooked road to **Ellington**, a small town of fewer than 1,000 residents and largely dependent on riverways tourism for income. The highway continues northward across open fields outside the confines of the **Mark Twain National Forest** before ducking back into the forest near **Centerville**, a very small town of steep hills, crooked streets, and modest but tidy houses. Centerville is also the seat of Reynolds County.

Five miles north of Centerville, the landscape, already rugged, becomes very rough indeed. The **St. Francois Mountains** are among the oldest in North America and are a remnant of a once-major range. Some geologists believe this range is the only one on the continent that was never submerged and existed as an island during periods of high water. This belief is based in part on the discovery of fossilized coral around the base of the mountains, but no coral has been found on the higher elevations.

Some facts and figures do indeed boggle the mind, such as this one: Geologists believe the range is somewhere in the vicinity of 1.4 billion years old and that what we see today are only the remnants of the mountains' roots. The Appalachians are about 460 million years old

© 2001 Missouri Division of Tourism

The Current River is one of the most popular rivers for float trips in the Midwest.

The Sandy Creek covered bridge is one of the best preserved bridges in the state, and is so popular that a park has been built around it.

and the Rockies are only 70 million years old. This means the St. Francois were already twice as old as the Appalachians are today when the Appalachians were a-borning. Mind boggling, indeed.

As an aside, forget about the French pronunciation. Missourians say Saint Francis, and they pronounce it saint rather than *sant*. Say *Sant* Louis and you'll get corrected.

MO 21 goes around the eastern side of this mountain barrier after merging briefly with MO 49, which turns northwest and goes around the western side of the range. Much of the mountain area that the two highways avoid is devoted to state parks and dead iron, lead, barite, zinc, silver, manganese, cobalt, and nickel mines. Throw in some limestone and granite quarries and you have a rich area.

The mountains are also the site of a hydroelectric project that was a marvel of engineering and conservation, and will be again in about 2009. This is the **Taum Sauk Pumped Storage Plant**, one of the few of its kind in existence when it was opened in 1963. The electric company AmerenUE built two reservoirs, one atop Profitt Mountain, with the other 800 feet below, and they dug a 7,000-foot tunnel to connect them. During the high-usage periods, the water turned the turbines as it went down to the lower reservoir; at night, when power requirements were much lower, the water was pumped back to the upper reservoir. Forty-two years after it opened, the upper reservoir failed. In the early morning of December 14, 2005, a triangular section gave way and more than a billion gallons of water were released that sent a 20-foot wall of water down the mountainside and into the Black River below. To everyone's surprise, there were no fatalities. Jerry Toops, superintendent of the Johnson's Shut-Ins and Taum Sauk State Parks, his wife, and their three children were swept some distance downstream in their home, but sustained only minor injuries.

The cause was twofold. A computer malfunctioned and allowed the reservoir to continue filling without shutting off, which caused the water to overflow. This combined with longstanding leaks in the reservoir walls, which weakened them, and the large section of the wall suddenly collapsed.

The power company has been building a new system and restoring the reservoir, and expects to resume operations in 2009.

Taum Sauk is a common place name in the mountains. It was the name of a legendary chief of the Piankishaw tribe. In the legend, his daughter Mina married an Osage warrior. The Piankishaw medicine man declared her bewitched and ordered her husband thrown from the highest mountain in the area to break the spell.

Mina was forced to watch her husband thrown from the mountain. She broke free from the women holding her, ran and jumped after her husband. The moment her body struck the rocks below, lightning flashed, thunder roared, and a stream poured out of the mountain and over their broken bodies.

The stream now is known as **Mina Sauk Falls**, which plunge 132 feet. It is an integral part of the **Taum Sauk State Park**, which also contains **Taum Sauk Mountain**. It is the highest point in Missouri, at 1,772 feet.

An odd thing about the legend is that the Piankishaw tribe was not known to live west of the Mississippi River. No matter. That is the name given the mountain, the waterfall, and the park.

This small mountain range holds two more state parks of note. **Johnson's Shut-Ins State Park** was badly damaged when the reservoir broke in 2005, and has been closed since. The anticipated reopening date is in 2008. How much the park has changed is not known. The park's name comes from a local euphemism for a canyon or gorge, called a shut-in.

© 2001 Missouri Division of Tourism

Johnson's Shut-Ins State Park is scheduled for reopening in 2008 after being severely damaged when the Tauk Sauk reservoir collapsed in 2005.

Elephant Rocks State Park protects a gathering of gigantic granite rocks, which have been eroded into rounded forms that look enough like circus elephants lined up trunk to tail to give the park its name. The park has trails among the rocks, including one about a mile long with signs in Braille. Another trail, without signs in Braille, leads to an old quarry where red granite was excavated in the 1880s.

A series of small towns are strung along MO 21 in this hilly area, including **Glover, Hogan, Arcadia, Ironton,** and **Pilot Knob.** Only Ironton has some heft as a community. It is quite small but has turned to antique shops as a survival tactic, giving the downtown area a cheerful look. Ironton also has several bed-and-breakfast inns and motels.

One spot on the map worth watching for is **Old Mines,** which is in the heart of the old mining district, and the source of a quaint entry in the Works Progress Administration (WPA) guidebook that was published in 1941. This guidebook was written in the 1930s while the area was still being mined by hand by a community of Creoles; some of them had been there for generations, enjoying their isolation from mainstream America.

The modern Creole works his garden plot desultorily, for his chief labor is digging ore. With the aid of his wife and children, he digs a shallow surface pit and from it scrapes enough tiff [another word for barite] to support a meager existence. When the ore is exhausted, or when the pit grows too deep to be worked by this primitive method, the spot is abandoned for a new one. Often the miner gathers enough ore during the first half of the week to permit him to hunt or fish or doze upon his galeire until the following Monday. French ballads and folk tales of the Middle Ages are popular, especially on holidays. On New Year's Eve, the young people stroll about the village, stopping at the homes of friends and singing "La Guignolee." The host usually serves cookies and wine. If he has nothing to give, his daughter must dance with the visitors.

Society has changed a bit since this was written, and one suspects most daughters today would have something firm to say about this custom.

The writer added that the village of Old Mines "was accumulated rather than founded," and wrote that it was believed that the first miner in the area was a Frenchman named Philippe Francois Renault, who was sent by the Company of Indies in about 1720. It is believed he established the first industry in Missouri, that of lead mining, with the work performed by paid employees and African slaves.

The iron and lead district continues north to **Potosi**, which was named for the Mexican mining town of San Luis Potosi (another mine by that name exists in Peru). The district is famous for having the largest known lead deposit in the world. Potosi is the only town of any size on this trip, and it has a Wal-Mart that redefines the word "large."

After leaving Potosi, MO 21 becomes suburban, with heavier traffic. The scenery is still nice but difficult to appreciate with a semi ahead and a tailgater behind. Before long, the road becomes urban as it crosses into the city limits of St. Louis.

IN THE AREA

Current River Heritage Museum, 101 Main Street, Doniphan. Call 573-996-5298. Among the exhibits are the world's largest sawmill, Civil War memorabilia, a one-room schoolhouse and a turn-of-the-20th-century kitchen. Open year-round. Free admission.

Parlor Bed and Breakfast, 203 S. Knob Street, Ironton. Call 866-550-6142. This B&B is surely the most unusual in the area, and in the entire state. It is in a former funeral home. Its limo is made of a 1974 Cadillac hearse. Proclaimed as one of Missouri's haunted inns, the owners insist that other places in the area are haunted as well. The carpenter-Gothic B&B also has a restaurant and offers carriage rides, if the hearse is a bit much for you. Web site: www.theparlorbandb.com.

Plain and Fancy B&B, Ironton. Call 888-546-1182. This B&B is 2 miles from Ironton on MO 72, in a 1908 farmhouse that has four guestrooms. Amenities include a hot tub, a gazebo, and a patio with fire pit. Not wheelchair accessible. Web site: www.plainfancybb.com.

Shepherd Mountain Inn, 1321 N. Route 21, Ironton. Call 573-546-7418. The inn has a Baylee-Jo's BBQ restaurant on the premises. Web site: www.shepherdmtninn.com.

Alexander W. Doniphan

Missouri historians are fond of claiming that their state is the mother of the West, and there is enough evidence to give the claim credence. Geography made the state's role in the Manifest Destiny inevitable. Here the Missouri and Mississippi Rivers converge, and here the overland routes westward had to begin for those arriving by the Mississippi, the Illinois, and the Ohio Rivers. It was the small end of the funnel through which settlers had to travel.

Two states in particular—Texas and New Mexico—are indebted to Missouri for their existence as part of the United States. Were it not for the First Missouri Volunteers, it is doubtful whether either state would have their present boundaries, and New Mexico might not exist at all. That tidy line from El Paso to the Pacific Ocean certainly would not exist. Missourians with some knowledge of history love to tease Texans about their debt to Missouri. Texans have a tendency to pretend they owe nothing to anyone other than their direct ancestors for securing the present boundaries of their state.

The episode referred to here—Alexander Doniphan's amazing march and battles—was bound up in the Manifest Destiny doctrine, a grandiose idea adopted by most Americans in the 1840s, which insisted that the country must expand from sea to sea. Preachers and politicians insisted that God had blessed the concept. Mexicans felt they had as much right to claim God as their partner in such endeavors, and their country was not cooperating at all with the *Norte Americanos*. Mexico wanted the land that it lost to the Texans back, and each time the two armies met, the Mexicans won decisively. Many Texas soldiers were killed and hundreds were taken prisoner and confined to horrible prisons throughout northern Mexico.

Enter Alexander Doniphan (1808–87), an attorney who would become one of Missouri's greatest heroes of the Mexican War. His exploits place him easily in the same company as another Missourian, General John J. "Black Jack" Pershing, of World War I fame. Before marching off to war, Doniphan had already distinguished himself as an attorney who was unafraid of unpopular causes by taking on the Mormons as clients. No religious group has been treated worse in the United States than the Mormons. They were expelled from Illinois, and soon after settling in north-central Missouri they were murdered at will. Doniphan had represented them, and had done a good job of it, despite personal threats. During this period, Doniphan enlisted in the U.S. Army as a private in 1846, but he was such a natural leader that he was quickly bumped up to the rank of colonel.

When the governor of Missouri declared his private war on the Mormons, Doniphan was promoted again, this time to brigadier general. The commanding officer of the war, Major General Samuel D. Lucas, sent Doniphan an order. Following is a record of the exchange between the two generals in *Doniphan's Epic March:*

> General Lucas. *To Brigadier-General Doniphan: Sir: You will take Joseph Smith and the other prisoners to the public square of Far West [a town that no longer exists] and shoot them at 9 o'clock tomorrow morning.*
>
> General Doniphan. *It is cold-blooded murder. I will not obey your order. My brigade shall march for Liberty tomorrow morning, at 8 o'clock; and if you execute these men, I will hold you responsible before an earthly tribunal, so help me God. A.W. Doniphan, Brigadier General.*

When the general received this reply, he apparently believed Doniphan because he did nothing.

According to Jeff Lindsay, a Mormon historian, "It is one of the very few times in American history when an officer refused on moral grounds to carry out the command of a superior without being called to account."

Doniphan was exceptionally tall for the period, standing 6 feet 4 inches; he stood eye to eye with Abraham Lincoln when they met. He knew how to deal with men to earn their loyalty and to get them to march up to 30 miles a day without hating him for it. He has often been called a natural warrior, in that he understood human psychology well enough to know what would and would not work on the battlefield, although he did not have any previous experience.

His volunteers came from 10 of the counties strung along the Missouri River between St. Louis and Kansas City. After they assembled and were given rudimentary training, they marched off down the Santa Fe Trail to fight in the Mexican War. Just getting to the war was almost too frightening to contemplate. The men had to ride and walk 900 miles to first reach Santa Fe. The trek took them three months. Once there, the battle everyone had anticipated did not happen. The Mexican army was nowhere in sight and Doniphan put his legal background to good use in Santa Fe to set up an American government. After giving his soldiers a chance to rest, get drunk if they wanted, and to become intimately acquainted with local women, Doniphan assembled them and headed due south toward El Paso, across 90 miles of terrible desert.

Before they arrived in El Paso, the Missourians engaged in a major battle at a place called Brazito, which was an old channel of the Rio Grande River. Here Doniphan displayed his genius for improvisation. He knew what kind of rifles the Mexican soldiers carried, and knew that their range was limited. When the Mexicans attacked, at each of their volleys Doniphan had several men fall into the tall grass as though killed or wounded. Nobody fired until the enemy was quite close; then, on Doniphan's command, all of the soldiers rose from their hiding places in the grass and began firing. The result was deadly for the Mexicans: their formation broke and the survivors ran for their lives.

This was the major battle of the expedition. More energy was expended just getting across the deserts than fighting. As they had in Santa Fe, the Missourians took El Paso with hardly a shot fired, and then marched south, deep into Mexico, contending with intense heat, shortages of water, sandstorms, and monotony. They fought another battle at a place called Sacramento with a Mexican army at least five times their size, and again won with very few casualties. They captured Chihuahua City and then marched eastward, an astonishing 600 miles to the Gulf of Mexico, arriving almost exactly a year after their departure from Missouri. At the gulf, the expedition caught a ship that took them to New Orleans. By this time, they were wearing rags and many were barefooted. But the soldiers followed Doniphan wherever he took them because by then he had shown his concern for them and his brilliance of leadership. Amazingly, only four men had been were killed up to this point.

In New Orleans, the soldiers were treated to the first of many displays of gratitude, with parades, parties, and long speeches. The victory lap continued up the Mississippi River to St. Louis, where they landed in June 1847.

Military experts have declared Doniphan's march one of the greatest in the history of warfare. One unidentified commentator, quoted in the WPA guide, said that the adventure was "one of the most brilliant long marches ever made; the force, with no quartermaster, paymaster, commissary, uniforms, tents or even military discipline, covered 3,600 miles by land and 2,000 by water, all in the course of 12 months."

After the Mexican adventure, Doniphan returned to his hometown of Richmond, Missouri, near Liberty, and lived quietly as a practicing attorney. When the Civil War broke out a decade and a half later, both the Union and Confederacy tried desperately to bring Doniphan onto their side. He refused. Like so many Missourians, and other border state residents, his loyalties were deeply divided. On the one hand, he could not bring himself to fight against the Union for which he had served so brilliantly before. Nor could he bring himself to fight against friends and relatives who favored the Confederacy. Another factor was his beloved wife's illness, and his brooding over the loss of two sons to sickness some years before. Doniphan sat out the war.

Doniphan's wife, Jane, died in 1873, although he lived on until 1887. A bronze 10-foot statue of him stands on the Ray County courthouse lawn, facing southwest.

Thayer to Cuba

Estimated length: 145 miles
Estimated time: all day

Getting there: From Thayer, on the Arkansas border, MO 19 goes north through Winona, Salem, Cuba, and Hermann. It continues northward and ends at Hannibal. This chapter describes the scenic designation from Thayer to Cuba.

Highlights: Seven of America's largest **springs, caves** and **disappearing rivers,** the **Ozark National Scenic Riverways, gristmills,** and **winding roads** through beautiful hardwood forests.

MO 19 is one of Missouri's most beautiful highways and goes through one of the state's most geologically interesting areas. The entire highway, from Thayer to Hannibal, is worth traveling, even though this trip ends at the Missouri River at Cuba. This section of road is special to most Missourians. There's hardly anyone in the state who hasn't paddled a canoe or rowed a boat down the Jacks Fork, Current River, or the Eleven Point River, or planned to or at least wanted to.

The highway begins at **Thayer,** right on the Missouri-Arkansas line. Thayer merges with the town of **Mammoth Spring** just south of the

© 2001 Missouri Division of Tourism

The Dillard Mill, near Davisville, is still in working order. The site is a popular picnic area as well.

border. The spring is part of the large system of underground rivers and resulting springs that make this area so interesting. Some riverbeds are caves, and several streams suddenly disappear into the earth and follow an underground route until they burst forth again as a cold, clear spring, all impurities removed by the underground limestone filtration system. This underground network is what created the gorge at **Grand Gulf State Park**, 6 miles west of Thayer. More than a mile of one cave's ceiling collapsed and created this gorge, with walls up to 130 feet high. One section of the ceiling remains standing as a natural bridge. The gorge is sometimes called the Little Grand Canyon. The area is open to visitors, but the park is still being developed, so facilities are modest at best.

This part of Missouri is almost entirely limestone, and it is laced with caves of all sizes. This is because limestone erodes so easily that a cross section of the earth's surface here would look like a honeycomb. Some of these caves are very large, and many have been turned into tourist attractions, such as the more than 30 caves in **Meramec State Park, Marvel Cave** near Branson, **Mark Twain Cave,** those in **Ha Ha Tonka State Park**, and **Onondaga** caverns. The largest collection of caves is in Perry County between **Ste. Genevieve** and **Cape Girardeau**. Perry County alone has 629 caves of all sizes. In 1990 the Missouri Department of Natural Resources recorded the 5,000th cave. Only Tennessee has more known caves.

When John Ashcroft was governor, in his pre–senatorial campaign/attorney general days, he immediately declared 1990 as "The Year of the Cave." In the past decade and a half, the number has grown to 6,200, with more being added frequently. The department says that, for the past 35 years, an average of 140 caves have been discovered annually throughout the state.

While driving on MO 19 between Thayer and **Winona**, you are likely to see more **garage sales** and **flea markets** than anywhere else in Missouri. In the warmer months, this area looks much like a stretched-out market. Roadside selling is one of the major forms of recreation in this area, and also a way to generate income while cleaning house and meeting new people. It seems that every fourth or fifth house along a country highway has a sign and a few tables with what some call "junktiques"—old electrical appliances, curtain rods, bottles and jars, picture frames, magazine racks, automotive accessories, and so forth. In many towns, these garage sales become flea markets on the main drag or by the main intersection.

Roadside sales are addictive, and aficionados will risk their safety, and yours, by making sudden and illogical decisions behind the wheel. They will park precariously on narrow shoulders, and they will intentionally drive into a deep ditch and worry about getting out later. At a garage sale, you may find yourself chatting with elderly men about the local football team, even though you have no idea where you are. Only the gregarious at heart have garage sales and fingering the used goods is a good way to kick-start a conversation.

The highway is prone to population explosions of lawn ornaments, and many front yards become zoos of miniature deer (never life-size because they might be used for target practice in—or out—of hunting season), ducks, squirrels, geese, and all manner of other small birds and beasts.

In 1984, after a long and often bitter dispute among environmentalists, loggers, miners, local businesses, and others, a 16,500-acre chunk of **Mark Twain National Forest** near Alton was designated as the **Irish Wilderness**, becoming the largest wilderness area in the state. It is an unusual wilderness area because it is all second-growth timber, having been logged off around the turn of the 20th century. But wilderness proponents felt that the forest deserved the designation because of its vastness and the feeling it gave visitors of being remote and mysterious.

There is another human story that is important to the wilderness. After the terrible potato famine in Ireland in 1848, many Irish fled to the United States, and more than 30,000 came to St. Louis, a staggering figure for the period. They were discriminated against all across the country, and St. Louis was no better because the power structure was composed of Germans and Anglo-Americans. The Irish were excluded. Women often could find work as domestics but their husbands and sons were usually forced to go on the road to seek work.

A priest, Father John Joseph Hogan, had a plan to alleviate this problem.

"A conscientious and idealistic pastor, Father Hogan despaired about effects on family life that inevitably resulted from the hard and difficult straits, and the forced separations, of his parishioners," James Denny, a parks operations officer for the Missouri Department of Natural Resources, wrote. "[Hogan] came to envision a solution to this social dilemma that was both bold and imaginative, yet quaint and utopian at the same time."

Hogan decided to found a settlement in the Ozarks, believing that if people worked hard and worked together, they could quickly build a viable community and become self-sufficient. The land was there for the taking, so Father Hogan led a group to the Eleven Point River near Alton, and they began clearing land and building their community. The plan looked promising.

But it was not to be. Several things went wrong with the plan. Father Hogan's hard-nosed efforts to turn the local residents into Catholics made them angry, and the local preacher even angrier. He launched an attack on the Irish community from his pulpit, which doomed the experiment in communal living. Then the Civil War broke out and its viciousness brought further grief to the Irish, and cleared them out of the area forever. Apparently, the last of the Irish—those who had not already left—were placed on a train filled with prisoners and refugees who were collected in the area in 1863 by a Union detachment.

By that time, Father Hogan was long gone. He was working in northern Missouri as a parish priest in Chillicothe. He never returned to the Ozarks. No trace of the Irish who tried to settle there was ever found.

Eleven Point River flows under MO 19 north of **Greer**, and it is Missouri's only designated **Wild and Scenic River**. It is a popular river with paddlers. Many put in at **Thomasville**, east of Greer, and float two or three days to emerge from the wilderness at **Riverton** on US 160. In Greer, a mile-long trail leads back to **Greer Spring**, which is the second largest spring in the state, so large that it doubles the size of Eleven Point River when it enters the river, and the spring's consistent flow makes the river navigable for boaters all year round.

The name Eleven Point is unusual and nobody is certain where it came from. One version has it that the first surveyors of the river had to keep changing their compass readings, and in one mile-long stretch had to change the readings 11 times because the river is so crooked.

It was in this area that a sad wildlife experiment was carried out in 1934. The Forest Service set aside 13,000 acres to conserve wildlife, such as deer, quail, and wild turkeys. An effort was made to reintroduce wild turkeys, which had been killed off to the brink of extinction—an experiment which proved to be a classic example of unintended consequences. The turkeys, famous for their ability to outsmart hunters, lost their wildness and became as tame as chickens. They nested in the worst possible places, and wolves, foxes, dogs, raccoons, opossums, and other critters treated their nests as a banquet. So a new plan was hatched, in a manner of speaking, and the turkeys were encouraged to remain afraid of everything.

Eminence is at the center of the Ozark National Scenic Riverways, which covers about 135 miles of the Current River and the tributary of Jacks Fork, which enters the Current a short distance below Eminence. The town was chosen as the county seat of Shannon County and was named for George "Peg-Leg" Shannon of the Lewis and Clark Expedition, who became a respected lawyer in northeastern Missouri. The town's name was also an honor for Shannon because it was named for his hometown in Kentucky.

The river and national park begin at **Montauk State Park**, where the Current River emerges from underground. The other branch of the park begins just upstream from Blue Spring on Jacks Fork. The park ends several miles downriver from **Van Buren**. The national park has more than 60 springs, including the appropriately named **Big Spring**, believed to be the largest single-outlet spring in the world. Another large spring is **Alley Spring**, where a two-story water-powered roller mill still stands.

These rivers needed a boat built especially for them, and the result was long and narrow with a flat bottom for clearing the shallows. The design that lasted was called a johnboat, in honor of the man who developed it for the White River. Trouble is, nobody can remember John's last name. In the late 1970s, a group of high school students from Lebanon, Missouri, working under the auspices of *Bittersweet* magazine, doing work which was on the order of the Foxfire folklore preservation project in the Appalachians, watched and helped a boat builder named Emmitt Massey construct a johnboat.

"Originally," Massey told the students, "they were built right on the riverbank. They were long. I've heard of some as long as twenty-seven feet to haul freight on the Current River. They were designed to be stable enough to stand upright in while fishing and to float in four inches of water."

Today few of the wooden johnboats remain. Aluminum has taken over because it is much lighter, more durable than wood, and cheaper. Several boatbuilding factories are scattered through the Ozarks, keeping the price down and availability high. Canoes are more popular than johnboats with visitors to the national park, and in all towns in the area you'll see stacks of canoes, looking almost like stacks of firewood, for rent. Nearby might be an old school bus that the rental firm uses to take customers to the river, and to bring them back from the river when they're through with their boat trip.

A typical winding blacktop road in the Ozark Mountains

MO 19 earns its scenic designation as it winds its way along the creeks and over the ridges to Eminence, Alton, Winona, and Salem. It is a great highway for sports cars, but not so great for anyone prone to carsickness, because it is almost entirely double yellow lined, either because of the curves or for steep hills. The highway is bordered by large blackjack and white oak, and in some places the trees form a canopy overhead. A few areas near the road have been logged off, but a screen of trees was left along the highway, easing the visual impact considerably. Cutting trees—the word harvesting doesn't seem to have found universal acceptance yet—brings howls and sighs of protest from many people. The irony is that many people who hate the thought of cutting a tree build new homes of wood, buy furniture made of wood, and burn wood in their stoves and fireplaces. It is the same as if a steak lover picketed slaughterhouses to force their closure.

However, this does not excuse what happened to the forest in this area. The wonder is that the forest has recovered as well as it has after being denuded of virtually every tree from the 1860s until around the turn of the 20th century. First, the timber companies took everything they could use and paid little or no attention to the aftermath. The hills were stripped of their cover and erosion was inevitable and severe.

When the timber companies moved on, several thousand employees chose to stay in the remote area to live off the land, and most lived as squatters on the tortured land. They tried to farm the hills but the land was stingy; it did not permit anyone to earn a living because its soil was far too shallow and washed away with every rain. Finally, the Forest Service stepped in with a management plan that included state parks, fish hatcheries, game preserves, and recreation areas. In the process the squatters were told to move on so the Forest Service could restore the land. During the Great Depression years of the 1930s, workers were brought in to stabilize the soil by replanting millions of trees, mostly oak and pine. The thick forests of straight oak and pine with dense underbrush that you see throughout the area today are a result of that government program during those hard years.

A small park and campground surrounds **Round Spring** north of Eminence, and although it isn't one of the largest springs in the region, it pours forth around 18 million gallons of water per day, which flows into the Current River about a quarter of a mile away. The spring comes out of the earth from a low, natural arch beneath a cliff. The area is dotted with caves.

In **Salem**, a pretty town with lots of brick homes and a four-story courthouse, you will see a sign outside a restaurant that tells you what part of the country you are in: It reads, parking out back. In most other parts of the country, the sign would have said, PARKING IN THE REAR.

About 23 miles north of Salem is the very small town of **Cherryville**, with a very large stone schoolhouse. Here you can turn east on MO 49 and drive about 12 miles down to the **Dillard Mill State Historic Site**. It is a pretty drive to the odd little town of **Dillard**, with only three or four homes, one with enough machinery parts out front to stock a parts store and the others as neat as that one is casual.

The mill is a mile from town on a dirt road that quickly becomes red clay, which is a challenge to drive on in the rainy season. The road winds along the banks of Huzzah Creek, and passes a few farms and a small cemetery before arriving at the mill.

Dillard Mill, which looks like an enormous red barn from a distance, was one of the last of the Missouri gristmills to go out of business. It was still grinding flour and meal until the 1960s because the area remained reasonably isolated. The original mill was built sometime before the Civil War and was known as Wisdom Mill for its owner, Francis Wisdom. He later sold it to Joseph Dillard Cotrell, whose middle name was selected as the name for the community, a name that later was changed to Davisville.

The next owner was Emil Mischke, who emigrated with his sister, Mary, from Poland. He bought the property, and in 1904 began building the present mill, using some timbers from the old mill. He blasted the millrace out of the limestone bluff and used a turbine rather than a waterwheel.

Mary Mischke became a partner in 1907, then sold her share to her brother 10 years later. Emil lived and worked alone for another decade but didn't like it, so he got himself a mail-order bride. This was during World War I and Missouri had many German immigrants, but after World War I, anti-German sentiment ran high. His wife had never liked life in the Ozarks, so in 1930, when some of his neighbors questioned Mischke's loyalty to the U.S., he sold the mill to Lester E. Klemme, moved to California, and never returned.

Klemme built rental cabins on the site and turned it into a resort called Klemme's Old Mill Lodge. He offered fishing in the millpond, and included meals in the $7 per day charge. He operated the mill for nearly 30 years before shutting it down for good in the 1960s. The state acquired the property, added several picnic areas, and now offers guided tours throughout the year.

Back on MO 19, you'll cross the Meramec River just north of **Steelville**. When you look down from the bridge on this free-flowing stream, think of all the Missourians who went to battle with the Corps of Engineers several years ago when the corps not only announced they were going to dam the river, but they had already started construction, before opponents were able to stop the proceedings. The Meramec is as pretty as the Eleven Point River and other widely promoted rivers in the Ozark National Scenic Riverways. It runs along high limestone bluffs and through timber and open fields on its way to the Mississippi, just south of St. Louis.

This journey ends at I-44 in **Cuba**, but feel free to continue north to the Missouri River at Hermann or the Mississippi at Hannibal to connect with routes described in other chapters.

IN THE AREA

Thayer only offers two modest places to sleep, so you might also check in Mammoth Springs, Arkansas, about 2 miles south of Thayer on US 63. Eminence is the unofficial capital city of the Ozark National Scenic Riverways, and as such it has the most places to sleep and eat. These range from full-fledged resorts to antiques-stuffed bed-and-breakfasts.

Aguila Lodge, Eminence. Call 573-226-5665. The lodge overlooks the Jacks Fork River and has 14 guestrooms, eight cabins, a steakhouse with a bar, and a game room. Please note pets are allowed but only with prior arrangement and steep fees apply. Web site: www.eminencelodge.com

Carr House Bed and Breakfast, 304 Chestnut Street, Thayer. Call 417-264-7771.

Coldwater Ranch Resort, Eminence. Call 573-226-3723. A restaurant is on the premises. Horse lovers are especially welcome and large box stalls are available for horses brought to the premises. Rides can be organized. Facilities include several cabins with queen-sized beds, full kitchen, and whirlpool tub. A bunkhouse with five beds, two bathrooms, and a full kitchen is available for groups. Web site: www.coldwaterranch.com.

Hawkins House Bed and Breakfast, 210 N. Main Street, Eminence. Call 877-875-7050. Three guestrooms are offered in this 1913 home. Full breakfast is served at the guest's convenience. Each room has a private bath with Jacuzzi, and king or queen beds. Web site: www.hawkinshaus.com.

Knapp House Bed and Breakfast, 410 S. Main Street, Eminence. Call 573-226-3131. Two guestrooms in the restored 1900 home have shared bath, and two cottages on the grounds have private baths. Full breakfasts are served. Children are welcome with prior arrangements.

OTHER CONTACTS

Dillard Mill State Historic Site. Call 573-244-3120. Web site: www.mostateparks.com/dillardmill.htm.

Ozark National Scenic Riverways, Van Buren. Call 573-323-4236. Web site: www.nps.gov/ozar.

The Odd Life of George Shannon

After the Lewis and Clark Expedition explorers' triumphant return to St. Louis in 1806, the men took their pay and scattered. Some returned to their homes in the eastern states, some went back up the Missouri River to become trappers and traders, and only one or two stayed in the Missouri area. One who stayed close to the expedition leaders was George Shannon, the youngest member of the group and probably the most intelligent, although there were times on the expedition when the leaders wondered.

Shannon was somewhere between 15 and 17 years old when he signed on with Captain Lewis in Kentucky. He was the eldest of nine children, and Lewis signed him on, along with Reubin and Joseph Field, in October 1803. Shannon's father had frozen to death the previous winter while hunting. Some historians believe that he and Lewis knew each other before this, but no firm evidence has surfaced.

In many ways, Shannon was a typical teenager who spent too much time daydreaming. The captains' journals mentioned the boy several times, sometimes to report that Shannon left something behind: a tomahawk, his gun, and powder and balls were among the items he left. His most celebrated adventure was when they were in the Dakotas and he was sent alone to search for two horses that had escaped during the night. He found them and went back to the river. There he saw some moccasin tracks on the river bank, assumed they belonged to the expedition members, and began following them. He was gone 12 days and the expedition members thought he had been killed. Instead, he and the two horses trudged onward until one of the horses grew too lame to keep up, but instead of killing him for food, Shannon set the animal free.

That was a mistake, because during those 12 days, Shannon had only one rabbit and some wild grapes to eat. He had killed the rabbit by loading his musket with powder and a stick and shooting with that, because he had expended all of his rifle balls in other, futile hunting attempts. He finally gave up the chase and sat down beside the river to wait for help from a trading boat that he believed would come by. Sometime. It was there the expedition found him, very weak and having to explain himself. A similar incident occurred on the return journey when he again was sent off alone to hunt and missed connecting back up with the main party. This time, he was lost only three days, and it wasn't his fault, just a misunderstanding among the men.

Except for these events and an occasional lapse of memory regarding his belongings, Shannon's name was mentioned in relation to his duties, which he performed well. Both captains were very fond of him and they kept him in St. Louis for almost a year after the expedition ended.

Shannon's life took a sudden and almost tragic turn in the spring of 1807 when he was hired as a hunter to accompany a party led by Nathaniel Pryor, who had been part of the expedition. Pryor, a sergeant during the expedition, was now an ensign, and he was ordered to return Sheheke, a Mandan chief, to his people in the Dakotas. The previous year the chief and a group of his people had joined Lewis and Clark on their return journey and went with them to St. Louis, then back to Washington, D.C., to meet President Jefferson.

Ensign Pryor's party, plus a fur trading party, left St. Louis in May for the arduous journey up the temperamental Missouri River. In September they were attacked by the Arikaras. The fighting was fierce, and eventually the Arikaras were driven off. Pryor then lashed his group's boats together and found that, while none of his men had been killed, three were wounded. The worst injury was Shannon's, whose leg was broken. Another man had been shot through the leg, but it was a clean wound, and the third had been wounded in the hip and arm.

Pryor turned around and headed for St. Louis, knowing it was futile to try to run the gauntlet the Arikaras would have for them. About a month later they were back in St. Louis, with Shannon barely alive and his wound a terrible mess. The doctor immediately amputated the leg above the knee and Shannon spent the next 18 months in the Army hospital near St. Louis. When he left the hospital, it was with a wooden peg-shaped leg, which earned him the nickname of Peg-Leg.

His former commanders made certain Shannon was paid for his trouble and loss by helping him obtain a pension for life. They also put him to work. The immense journals the captains had kept were placed in the hands of a writer named Nicholas Biddle, who had been chosen to prepare the first official version of the expedition. Biddle was in Philadelphia, so Shannon went there in 1811 to help him; Biddle spoke very highly of Shannon's ability to interpret the captains' journals and in supplementing their entries with his own account of the expedition.

After this assignment ended, Shannon read law, passed the bar in Kentucky, and in 1818 became a circuit judge. He was elected to the Kentucky House of Representatives in 1820 and 1822. But his tenure in the Kentucky legal system was cut short when he granted a new trial to the governor's son, who had been convicted of murder and sentenced to hang. The fact that the governor had appointed Shannon to the lifetime judgeship may or may not have been instrumental in this decision. The public was outraged, and it wasn't long before Shannon packed up his wife and moved to Missouri in 1828. There he was made a U.S. attorney in 1830, but when he was eligible for another four-year term, his nomination was withdrawn for no given reason.

In the meantime, Shannon became known as an excellent defense lawyer and a compulsive practical joker. Some of his jokes became legends along the Mississippi and Missouri Rivers. Here are three examples from *Nine Young Men from Kentucky:*

> He played a game of "horse" with a friend, daring him to do anything he, Shannon, would do, and if he did not he must buy a round of drinks for the house. Shannon immediately unstrapped his wooden leg and threw it into the fire.

> While spending the night at a country tavern, and drinking heavily, he became annoyed at the noisy ticking of a clock, told it to shut up several times, and when that didn't work, he shot it dead with his pistol. The next morning he saw what he had done and paid the innkeeper for it.

> Finally, perhaps his most dangerous prank was when he became angry with a state senator when both were staying in the Stone Hotel in Jefferson City. Shannon kept plying the senator with booze until he was very drunk. Shannon led him to the Missouri River, put him into a small boat, and then he pushed it out into the stream. The snoring senator drifted about 15 miles downriver and finally landed on a sandbar, where he was eventually rescued.

Shannon died quite suddenly on August 23, 1936, while in Palmyra to defend a man accused of murder. Eulogies were printed by the score. He was buried in Palmyra, but all traces of the cemetery have been obliterated.

St. Louis to Hermann

Estimated length: 70 miles
Estimated time: all day

Getting there: Driving west from St. Louis, this trip takes in towns on the north and south banks of the Missouri River, along MO 100 on the south bank and MO 94 on the north bank.

Highlights: Missouri's major **wine district**; historic towns of **Washington, Hermann, Labadie,** and **St. Albans**; lots of bed-and-breakfast inns; European-style **festivals**.

Most of us are partial to trips that begin in a large city, but would rather do without driving white-knuckled down an interstate amid drivers who probably know where they're going while we don't. This is a good trip for anyone suffering from interstate phobia because it begins by meandering westward out of St. Louis on Manchester Boulevard. Just beyond the city limits, Manchester Boulevard drops by the wayside and MO 100 takes over and doesn't stop until Jefferson City.

Long before the state's capitol appears, you will encounter an area with deep ties to Germany. Consequently, the region has become known as **Missouri's Rhineland**. It is a good name because a touch of the Old World

This small house in Labadie is typical of the homes built in the 19th century, complete with the front porch that became so popular in the U.S.

is strung along the last 100 miles of the Missouri River before it joins the Mississippi in St. Louis. Oak and walnut trees cover the low hills, and row crops march across the rich bottomlands. Towns with sturdy buildings made of limestone and brick perch on the high bluffs along the southern bank of the river. Lutheran churches are usually as tall as their Catholic competitors, and homes and businesses are so well built that it would take a major catastrophe to demolish them.

Although little known outside of Missouri until lately, this is one of the major winemaking areas of the Midwest. Some of the oldest wineries in America were established here. In one of those oddities of history, wine grapes grown here were responsible, in a negative way, for changing the entire French wine industry. More on that later.

Hermann is the focal point of the Rhineland. Other German-settled towns stand farther west, such as **Starkenburg** and **Westphalia**, and ethnographic maps of Missouri show German settlements all over the state, but Hermann represents the most ambitious attempt to retain 19th-century German culture. Lately, it has been the most active in promoting the preservation of Missouri's German heritage, and more than 100 of its buildings are on the National Register, which include most of the buildings in this small town of less than 3,000 in population.

Hermann was founded in 1837 by members of the Philadelphia Settlement Society, an organization of German immigrants who set out to establish a colony in the remote western parts of the country that would carry out the ideals of German nationalism. The society bought 11,000 acres in Missouri and sold off lots to its members. These newcomers were so well educated that locals nicknamed them the *Lateinische Bauern* (Latin peasants).

This learning is reflected in names they gave the town and its streets. Hermann was named in honor of Hermann Arminius, the German warrior whose armies defeated Caesar Augustus's forces in the Battle of Teutoburg in the year A.D. 9, and forced them back from the Elbe River to the Rhine. Hermann settlers named streets after Mozart, Beethoven, Goethe, Gutenberg, and Schiller. In a direct challenge to Philadelphia, when they laid out Hermann they made the main street 10 feet wider than Philadelphia's main boulevard.

Grapes were one of the first crops the settlers planted because they found that the soil and climate were similar to that of their homeland. The first grapes matured in 1845, and in 1846 the vineyards produced 1,000 gallons of wine. Soon wine was the major product in the area, and by 1893 **Stone Hill Winery** in Hermann was the third largest winery in the world. The largest was in Europe; the second largest was the Lonz Winery in Ohio. Happily, both the Lonz and Stone Hill wineries still exist.

Like wineries everywhere in America, those in Missouri suffered a severe blow when Prohibition put an end to commercial winemaking in the 1930s. All of Hermann's wineries closed; Stone Hill was converted to growing mushrooms. It continued doing so until 1965, when a local couple, Jim and Betty Held, bought the whole operation, got rid of the mushrooms, and began making wine again. Today Stone Hill is perhaps the best known of Hermann's wineries; it stands on a high hill overlooking Hermann and the Missouri River. Founded in 1847, it has a series of cellars, supposedly the largest in America, which are shown on tours. The tasting room sells wine, gifts, and food items. The winery's **Vintage 1847 Restaurant** is open for lunch and dinner.

Downtown on First Street is another winery, the **Hermanhoff**, established in 1852, five years after Stone Hill. A National Historic Site, it has a large main building and the **Festhalle**. Tours visit the 10 stone-and-brick–arched cellars and the smokehouse where German sausages are made. Picnickers are welcome in the courtyard. Next door is an **Amish country store** with handmade gifts.

Several of Hermann's beautiful homes, built by vintners before Prohibition, have been turned into bed-and-breakfasts. The largest is the three-story Victorian brick mansion called **Birk's Goethe Street Gasthaus**, which was built by the owner of Stone Hill Winery. Elmer and Gloria Birk worked several years restoring and furnishing the home before Elmer's untimely death. The inn offers "mystery" weekends (actors perform a mystery while visitors try to solve it), which run Friday through Sunday on the first two full weekends of each month. Reservations well in advance are essential for the mystery weekends, and recommended at other times.

Another popular bed-and-breakfast is the **Schmidt Guesthouse**, owned by Mimi Schmidt, who helped found the annual Maifest in 1952, and who is now director of Hermann's Showboat community theater. Her B&B is small—only two to four guests—and intimate, and she enjoys showing guests around her native town.

Hermann also claims the distinction of having the only courthouse in Missouri built with private funds. When a local wealthy citizen, Charles D. Eitzen, died, he left $50,000 to build the **Gasconade County Courthouse**.

Hermann has several celebrations throughout the year, and is well equipped for large crowds; its **Beer Hall** is said to be the largest in the world. The major festivals are the **Wurstfest** on the third weekend of March, the **Maifest** on the third weekend of May, the annual **antiques market** on the third weekend of June, the **Great Stone Hill Grape Stomp** the second Saturday of August, the **Volksmarch** on the third weekend of September, the **Oktoberfest** every weekend in October, and an old-fashioned **Christmas celebration** in December.

Wine has become more and more important in Missouri's Rhineland, and about a dozen wineries are scattered within sight of the Missouri River between Hermann and St. Louis. Oddly, the relatively small region supports two viticultural areas, Hermann and **Augusta**. The latter was the first such area designated in America after the United States. Treasury Department established the system in 1983, modeled after those in France. Although Hermann is the centerpiece of the Rhineland, the rest of the area on both sides of the Missouri down to St. Louis has good restaurants, inns, bed-and-breakfasts, and of course, several wineries. About half a dozen wineries are on the north side of the Missouri, from St. Louis to the small town of **Portland** northwest of Hermann on MO 94. (You can cross the river on MO 19 in Hermann, then head west on MO 94 to Portland.) The **Green Valley Vineyards**, in Portland, makes wine from French hybrid grapes grown on 15 acres of land and specializes in dry and semidry wines.

Blumenhof Vineyards is in **Dutzow**, a picturesque town downriver on MO 94 with rolling hills and steep timber. The vineyard specializes in dry table wines.

A short distance downriver is **Augusta**, one of those little places that sat virtually ignored for decades until the Rhineland started coming into its own. Augusta was built on the banks of the Missouri, but one spring, many years ago, the river shifted its course 2 miles away and stayed there. The funky, ramshackle little town was left high and dry on a low hill overlooking rich bottomland. Although it was one of the towns damaged by the 1993 flooding, Augusta has become an arts-and-crafts center and has three wineries: **Mount Pleasant, Cedar Ridge,** and **Montelle**.

To visit more of the Rhineland on the south side of the river, cross back on MO 19 into Hermann, then head east on MO 100. A few miles outside **Washington** is the **Sunny Slope Winery** in a brick home that dates back to the Civil War. The winery is set in a vineyard where French hybrid grapes are grown.

Vidal grapes

Farther down the Missouri River toward St. Louis are other wineries and historic towns. Most of Washington sits on a bluff even higher than Hermann. Beautiful buildings range from the sturdy German-design brick and stone homes to the Victorian mansions on the hills. For nearly a century, the town has been known for two factories: one that made excellent zithers around the turn of the century, and another which has turned out millions of corncob pipes. The **Missouri Meerschaum Co.** opened for business in 1869. The company was General Douglas MacArthur's sole supplier of the distinctive pipes with a $4^1/2$-inch-tall bowl and long stem. Other famous customers were General John J. Pershing, President Gerald Ford, President Dwight D. Eisenhower, and Carl Sandburg.

The pipes are made from a type of corn developed by the University of Missouri to produce a thick, tough cob, and the company contracts with several farmers to grow the cobs for them. The farmers get to keep the corn and are paid per acre of cobs grown. This guarantees the company a steady supply of cobs so they can keep their production at an average of 7,000 pipes per day.

Most of Washington's riverfront buildings have been restored and turned into offices, shops, and restaurants. Although Washington is located in a very hilly area—all towns on the south side of the river are—it is a pleasant town for walking.

Some of the towns along this stretch of the river have remained small, hardly more than a cluster of buildings. **Labadie** is a row of Victorian homes and false-front store buildings. **St. Albans**, one of the oldest towns in the state, is near a cave described at some length by Lewis and Clark in the journals from their journey to the Pacific. It was near here that Captain Lewis nearly fell off a 300-foot cliff and barely managed to catch himself after falling about 20 feet. All of St. Albans' few buildings are elegant in a turn-of-the-century way, and all, including the post office, were at one time owned by one family, the Johnsons, who also owned the International Shoe Company. In 1988 the Johnson family decided to sell the town and an organization called St. Albans Properties LLC was formed to buy it, all 5,400 acres of it. They formed the Country Club of St. Albans and began selling lots for homes. Today houses that sell for $2 million are common.

St. Albans is an upscale town with a resort atmosphere and is noted for its friendly, relaxed citizens. You'll see an inordinate number of sports cars in and around the town, and most people drive slowly through the small village, slower than the posted speed limit.

One of the nicest characteristics of Missouri's Rhineland is that the area has a lived-in look: it isn't a series of "theme" villages designed to attract visitors. You will share the narrow highways with tractors pulling manure spreaders, and a few farmers still use horses for some fieldwork. When you go into a hardware store, you will find nuts and bolts, barbed wire, 10-penny nails, horseshoe nails, and axle grease. You probably won't find postcards and T-shirts. At the post office, you'll see groups of men in overalls and gumboots standing around talking about Catawba grapes and Chenin Blanc as though wine is just another local product, like corn or hay. Which, of course, it is.

IN THE AREA

At last count, more than 50 bed-and-breakfast inns were open in the Hermann area, most in large historic homes. To list all of them, plus the restaurants, would require enough space for a separate book on the Hermann area alone. At least two dozen restaurants in Hermann serve everything from Cajun to Tex-Mex to French and German dishes. You are urged to contact the Hermann Chamber of Commerce for information on lodging, dining, wineries, and special events.

Adam Puchta Winery, 1947 Frene Creek Road, Hermann. Call 573-486-5596. Web site: www.adampuchtawine.com.

Augusta Winery, Augusta. Call 660-228-4301 or 888-MOR-WINE. Web site: www.augustawinery.com.

Bias Winery & Gruhlke's Microbrewery, Berger. Call 573-834-5475. Web site: www.biaswinery.com.

Birk's Goethe Street Gasthaus, 700 Goethe Street, Hermann. Call 573-486-2911 or 888-701-2495. This is one the best examples of what you can expect for lodging in Hermann and one of the largest B&Bs in the area. Well-behaved children allowed on weekdays only (Sun–Thu). No pets. Web site: www.birksgasthaus.com.

Blumenhof Vineyards, Dutzow. Call 314-433-2245. Web site: www.blumenhof.com.

Hermann Hill Vineyard and Inn, 711 Wein Street, Hermann. Call 573-486-4455. This very German building stands on the rim of a high hill overlooking Hermann. It has the extravagant high ceilings associated with

Rhine mansions, tall French doors, stained glass, and dark woodwork throughout. The inn has eight guestrooms, all with a fireplace, oak sleigh beds, private baths and whirlpool tubs, and private balconies. All guests must be at least 18 years old. No pets. Web site: www.hermannhill.com.

Hermannhof Winery, 330 E. First Street, Hermann. Call 314-486-5959. Web site: www.hermannhof.com.

Stone Hill Winery, Route 1, Hermann. Call 314-486-2221. Web site: www.stonehillwinery.com.

Vintage 1847 Restaurant at **Stone Hill Winery,** Hermann. Call 573-486-3479. Open daily. Lunch from 11 AM; dinner from 5 PM.

OTHER CONTACTS

Hermann Area Chamber of Commerce. Call 314-486-2313. Web site: www.hermannmo.com.

The Louse That Roared

On the campus of a small agricultural college in Montpellier, France, stands a statue of a young woman, depicting the United States, comforting an elderly woman, who represents Europe. The statue commemorates one of the most unusual events in the history of winemaking, and serves as a reminder that, for much of the 19th century and until the Prohibition era of the 1920s, Missouri was the dominant wine-producing area of North America and Hermann was the center of the industry.

During Hermann's heyday, Stone Hill Winery was only one of more than sixty wineries in the area, and together these wineries produced more than 3 million gallons of wine each year. Most of it was poured into oak casks and taken by boat downriver to St. Louis to be bottled and sold.

In the midst of this American success story came the chain of events that changed the wine industry in Europe, and established a connection between the Old World and the wilderness of the New World. It started when wines from Missouri began overshadowing European wines at international competitions. Partly from curiosity and partly to fight fire with fire, French vintners began importing rootstock from America to experiment with the grapes themselves.

Nobody knew until it was too late that the American vines carried a member of the aphid family called Phylloxera. The tiny pest, native to the

Statue on Montpellier, France, campus honoring Missouri wine experts

United States, is not much larger than a grass seed. It attacks the roots of grape vines, but the American vines had built up a resistance to the insect and nobody was even aware of its existence until the pioneer entomologist Asa Fitch (1809–79) studied it and named it after observing the damage it caused on European vines brought to America. It also attacked American grape roots native to America, but the roots healed quickly and no aftereffects were noted. The foreign vines brought over from Europe did not have this immunity. They inevitably died.

Once the tiny monster arrived in France, it began systematically destroying the vineyards. The plague rapidly spread across France and, by the 1860s, the majority of French vineyards were destroyed or severely damaged. The plague also crossed into Spain and showed up in Great Britain. Nobody knew the cause and it wasn't until decades later that they found the pest could be transported easily from one area to another, sometimes clinging to the soles of shoes or boots or caught in the cuffs of pant legs.

The pest brought the French wine industry to its knees. Only small, isolated parts of France escaped, but the wine industry was changed forever. Many vintners had to give up and begin growing row crops, assuming that winemaking was dead. This was the period when Scotch whiskey came into its own; it was often used as a substitute for French brandy.

Eventually the cause was detected, and not long after that a solution was discovered. All the men involved in finding the solution were recent immigrants to America. The first inkling of an answer came from two entomologists in St. Louis. Charles V. Riley was born in England and immigrated to the United States in the early 1860s. He settled in Illinois and worked as a farmhand, but he was fascinated with insects and soon became recognized as an expert.

When word of the Phylloxera disaster came to Missouri, Riley and George Englemann, a German-born viticulturalist, quickly determined that it was not possible to eradicate the insect once it was established. Instead, they had to learn how to live with it, and the only way was to graft French vines onto the immune American rootstocks.

Two more Missourians entered the story at this time to test the grafting on several varieties of grape. One was a winemaker from Neosho, Missouri, named Hermann Jaeger. He was born in Switzerland in 1844 and learned the wine business while working for a wine house near Lake Geneva. Jaeger immigrated to the United States in 1864 and settled in Neosho, Missouri. He bought 40 acres, a brother bought an adjoining 40 acres, and they began growing grapes and experimenting by grafting Concord and Virginia vines onto the wild grapevines. It is said that Jaeger originated more than 100 varieties of grapes.

The fourth person was George Husmann, a University of Missouri professor who was born in Germany and came to the United States with his parents in 1836. Soon he was growing grapes; Husmann helped found the 1,700-acre Bluffton Winery in Bluffton, Missouri. He went on to become a professor of forestry and viticulture at the University of Missouri, and wrote a classic book, *Grape Growing and Wine Making*.

Husmann and Jaeger worked together on the problem and they found that Riley and Englemann's recommendations were the key. They had found a cure for the plague. Grafting the more sensitive vines onto hardy American rootstocks created immunity to the louse. An estimated 10 million rootstocks, mostly *Vitis riparia* and *Vitis rupestris* grown in nurseries in Neosho and Sedalia, were shipped to France.

While these Missourians literally saved the French wine industry, the episode also radically changed the way the French produced wine thereafter. After the vineyards were destroyed, many farmers began growing other crops that required less of an investment of money and time. Wheat, corn, and many other crops are easier to grow than wine grapes. Most large vineyards were consigned to history and the smaller ones, sometimes called boutique wineries, became much more specialized. Rather than covering hundreds of acres, they became much smaller, with quality and individuality becoming more important than quantity. Consequently, French wines became better than ever before. Down in Texas, an agriculturalist named Thomas Volney Munson arrived at the solution at the same time as the Missourians, and he worked with the brandy producers in Cognac, France.

The French were grateful for the Missouri rootstocks and unashamed to admit it. On January 1, 1889, the French government bestowed the Cross of the Legion of Honor on Hermann Jaeger because of his dominant role in the successful experiment. The statue of a young woman holding an older woman, pictured on page 130, was erected on the campus of the Ecole Nationale Superieure Agronomique in Montpellier, with a plaque thanking the Missouri wine industry for saving the French vineyards. Interestingly, Missouri grapes are still not affected by Phylloxera because they had developed an immunity.

Of the acclaimed and decorated wine industry heroes, three of the four led long and productive lives. After an illustrious career as a professor and winemaker in Missouri, George Husmann accepted an offer from the Talcoa Winery in California's Napa Valley, where he worked several years performing his magic on vines. Later, he bought the Oak Glen Winery in the Chiles Valley and operated it until his death in 1902. Husmann's books remained in print for many years, and one of his quotes about wine is still widely reprinted today. Speaking of Zinfandel, he wrote, "I have yet to see the red wine of any varietal, which I would prefer to Zinfandel produced in California. Unfortunately, the BEST samples are like angels visits, few and far between." As an aside, Husmann's beloved Chiles Valley became the 80th designated viticultural area in 1999.

Charles Riley went on from success to success. Although he did not have a university education, he was made a professor and eventually was given an honorary Ph.D. from the University of Missouri. He later became chief of the U.S. Department of Agriculture's Bureau of Entomology and was later curator of insects at the U.S. National Museum.

Little is known about George Englemann other than that he continued his work in entomology. Unlike the others, he disappeared from the research scene.

Hermann Jaeger, the most honored of the group, did not have a happy life. He returned from France to his home in southwest Missouri and continued his work. A reclusive man, he had few local friends but did maintain a correspondence with other horticulturalists, publishing articles in journals all over the world. But he suffered from migraines and apparently had emotional problems as well.

In 1895, six years after receiving the Cross of the Legion of Honor, Jaeger told his wife he was going to Joplin. Sometime later his family received an undated letter postmarked in Kansas City, saying he "wanted to make an end to it before I get crazy" and asked them not to look for him. No trace of him was ever found.

Today Missouri winemakers are especially fond of telling a possibly apocryphal story about what happened when California growers needed a supply of root stock after its vineyards began dying of the root louse: Rather than going to Missouri for their supply, the vintners in California imported the Missouri root stocks from France. Missourians like to say the Californians couldn't bear the thought of getting their replacement vines from Missouri.

CHAPTER

11

Arrow Rock to Fort Osage

Estimated length: 120 miles
Estimated time: all day

Getting there: From I-70 at Boonville, in central Missouri, take MO 41 west to Marshall, then west to US 24 into Lexington.

Highlights: Historic **Arrow Rock** and **Lexington**, one of Missouri's major Civil War battlefields, and **Fort Osage**.

This trip is a good alternative to cruising across Missouri on I-70 sandwiched between semis going 75 miles an hour and following you so close that all you see is the chrome of their bumper and grill. The distance between Boonville and Kansas City on this route isn't that much greater than on I-70, but the traveling conditions are much better. This route offers rolling hills with alternating timber and crops, and two historic towns.

The area around **Boonville** is rich in Native American and Civil War history. A small town northwest of Boonville named **Arrow Rock** is one of the most historically interesting towns in the area, in part because it still looks so much like it did when it came into being. The boulder now known

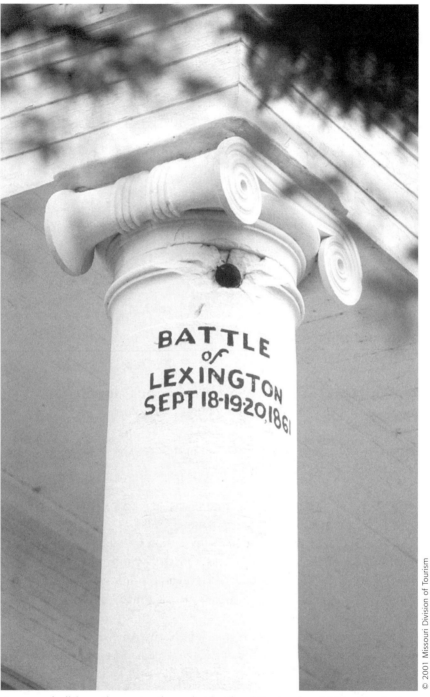

© 2001 Missouri Division of Tourism

A cannonball from the major three-day battle of September 1861 at Lexington remains lodged in a column that supports the front of the courthouse.

as Arrow Rock is one of the earliest landmarks noted by explorers on the Missouri River. The first maps were by French cartographers who called the landmark Pierre a Fleche, for the very good reason that it means arrow rock in French. They apparently heard it called that by Native Americans in the area who used its stone for arrowheads. It was such a distinct landmark that everyone who went by mentioned it in writing, including those in the Lewis and Clark Expedition.

The first trading post was established in 1813 by George Champlain Sibley. Sibley abandoned the post a year later because of the increase in Native American raids, moving downriver to St. Charles. Although Sibley's Fort and Trading Post at Arrow Rock didn't last long, it was an impressive structure. It was of traditional blockhouse design with a two-story main building that measured 20 by 30 feet. It was made of cottonwood logs with an oak slab roof. A log stockade surrounded it.

Arrow Rock became busier as the route from St. Charles heading west became a trail, then a road called Boone's Lick (or Booneslick) Road. It ran to Old Franklin, across the river from where Boonville stands now. This became the launching point for the Santa Fe Trail, which was started by William Becknell when he made his historic round-trip journey to Santa Fe in 48 days. This trail began at Old Franklin, went upriver a short distance to Arrow Rock, then left the river and turned north on a long loop, and headed straight for Fort Osage near Independence. Here the Santa Fe, California, and Oregon Trails converged, and then went their separate ways again. In later years, the Santa Fe Trail officially began downriver at Independence, 780 miles from Santa Fe.

All of this became history once the transcontinental railroads were built. Like nearly every town that depended on trails, Arrow Rock became only a shadow of its former self.

The town's most famous citizen was the artist George Caleb Bingham, now considered one of the greatest American painters of the 19th century. Bingham had no formal training. He appears to be one of those geniuses who didn't need to study. He needed an easel, paint, and brushes, and little else. The only known instruction Bingham received occurred, when he was nine: he watched the painter Chester Harding paint a commissioned work in Arrow Rock.

Bingham's parents were married in their home state of Virginia. His mother's father gave his parents a mill and a 1,180-acre estate with several slaves, but with the agreement that the father could live on the land the rest of his life. The father also still held ownership, and when a friend needed a loan he put up the estate as collateral. The friend died before he could make good on the debt, and all was lost. So the Binghams moved to Franklin, Missouri, near Boonesville, because they had heard the land was fertile and cheap.

By the time George was born, in 1811, his father was a judge. When George was 12, his father died of malaria. His mother opened a school for girls where George was the janitor. As George matured, he apprenticed with two cabinetmakers, both Methodist ministers, and he did some preaching himself.

But painting was the stronger desire, and at 19 he was painting portraits for $20 each, sometimes completing one in a single day. They were the work of a master, and he became so popular that nearly everyone in the Arrow Rock area had to have one on their walls in order to prove that they had good taste. One source said, "Not to have a Bingham on the wall was as rare as not to have a Bible on the center table."

With this success, Bingham decided to move to St. Louis where there were wealthy people who would pay much more than $20 for a portrait. Just before he left, he came down with the measles. When he recovered, he was permanently bald. But his popularity spread and he never lacked for an income the rest of his life. He married three times—his first two wives died while quite young—and he had three children. In later years, Bingham became interested in politics and in 1848 he was elected to the Missouri assembly; he also served in several appointed positions, and was a professor of art at the University of Missouri in Columbia. Bingham died in 1879.

Bingham's best-known painting shows an old and a young man on a canoe with some kind of small animal on the bow. The painting is evocative of the fur trading days, and of a much simpler time. Bingham's name for it, *French Trader, Half-breed Son*, was changed by the politically correct American Art Union to *Fur Traders on Missouri River*.

In 1873 Arrow Rock was partly destroyed by a fire set by three young arsonists, who were arrested, then lynched before a trial could be held. Another fire in 1901 caused extensive damage to the downtown district. By then the town had been consigned mostly to history and as a place for local people to shop. Its glory days as an outfitting post for the trek west were gone forever.

With a population that hovers around 100, Arrow Rock has remained both small and historic, and those liabilities have helped make the town famous. The restoration program began when the Daughters of the American Revolution (DAR) took on the Old Tavern as a project in 1912. A decade later, the Missouri legislature purchased the tavern so the DAR could continue its restoration, which in turn led to the creation of **Arrow Rock State Park** in 1926. The park was further improved in the 1930s by a Works Progress Administration project.

The Friends of Arrow Rock was formed in 1959 and raised funds to restore the old courthouse, the International Order of Odd Fellows lodge hall, the gun shop, and some other buildings. Nearly every building in town has a name and its history in print.

One of the most popular buildings is **George Caleb Bingham's home,** where he resided from 1837 until he moved away in 1845. The house at the end of High Street was declared a National Historic Landmark in 1968, after being restored by the Missouri Park Department.

Next door to the Bingham house is a large depression in the bluff that separates the town from the Missouri River. It is called Godsey's Diggin's in honor of the man in charge of a public works project that was never completed. The town fathers decided to dig a channel from the river into the heart of town so that wharves and warehouses would be more easily accessed by riverboats and barges. The work continued off and on from 1840 until 1857, but the town has only the man-made ravine to show for the project.

One of the most imposing houses in the area is known as the **Sappington House.** It stands on Route TT just west of Arrow Rock. It was built by Dr. John Sappington, who invented Sappington Anti-fever Pills, using quinine as a cure for malaria, one of the most common ailments in those years. In an act of great generosity, Sappington gave away patent rights to the pills rather than collecting a royalty, so that the medicine would be more affordable to everyone. One of Sappington's grandsons became governor of Missouri and two of his sons-in-law held the same office. He was also the great-great-great-grandfather of the wonderful dancer and actress Ginger Rogers.

For a century, several small huts remained standing behind the Sappington House as a reminder of a part of Missouri's past that most of us today wish had never happened. The huts were slave quarters. Recently, a resident of Arrow Rock said that only one of the huts remains today.

Every town needs a witty character: it is hard to imagine any town that can be considered interesting without a quotable personality. Dr.

Sappington was up to the task. He believed in being prepared for the inevitabilities of life, so while he was still in perfect health he purchased a coffin and shoved it under his bed. Not one to waste space, the doctor used it as a place to store fruit and nuts, which he always served his grandchildren when they visited.

Sappington had three comely daughters. Clairborne F. Jackson, who became governor of Missouri, married one of the daughters, but she died young. Jackson liked the family so he married another of the young Sappington women. Alas, she died as well. Not one to give up on a family, Jackson came back for the third. "You can take her," Papa Sappington told the persistent suitor, "but don't come back after the old woman."

Arrow Rock's **Lyceum Theater** is Missouri's oldest professional theater. Built as a Baptist church in 1872, the population dwindled, which meant churches either closed or merged. The Baptists joined another congregation and the church was eventually abandoned. Fortunately, the building remained standing and was used for a variety of purposes over the next 90 years. In 1960 a local group founded a theater in the old church, and they hired a professor at the then Christian College in Columbia, Henry Swanson, as artistic director. As an aside, the original lyceum was a school, or gymnasium, near Athens, Greece, where Aristotle taught.

After 19 years at the theater, Swanson retired and was replaced by Michael Bollinger, who stayed on the job 25 years and greatly expanded the theater's repertoire, influence, and fame. Attendance ballooned to 24,000 a year in 2004. The year Bollinger took over, 1979, attendance was only 6,900.

The theater company hires professional equity actors and performs a selection of musicals, comedies, and dramas throughout the summer and into the autumn, June until October. Arrow Rock has responded by now offering a number of bed-and-breakfasts, some only one or two rooms, a variety of places to eat, antique stores, and gift shops. Fortunately, most of the downtown buildings have a lived-in look versus the perfectly preserved appearance of buildings that give national and state parks such a sterile atmosphere. After all, when you walk into a 200-year-old store, you expect to see at least some uncataloged junk and at least a whiff of mustiness and mildew.

MO 41 continues on to **Marshall**, a small city of about 12,000 with an emphasis on manufacturing and agriculture. The route to **Lexington** is west on US 65 to Waverly, then west on US 24, which continues through Lexington to Kansas City.

Lexington was founded by migrants from Lexington, Kentucky, and has about 5,000 residents. The biggest event in its history was a three-day Civil War battle that ended on September 20, 1861.

Lexington became an important river port when the Civil War broke out. Most of its citizens had pro-South leanings, but those who were uncertain which side to support had their doubts erased when the Union soldiers came to town in September 1861 and took nearly $1 million from the local bank. A few days later, the Missouri Guard arrived in pursuit of the Yankees and a lot of money. The Battle of Lexington began.

This battle, considered one of the major battles fought in Missouri, was between the Missouri State Guard, under the command of Major General Sterling Price, and the Union troops, under Colonel James A. Mulligan. Some call the conflict the Battle of Hemp Bales because bales of the material were used as movable breastworks. The Confederates soaked the bales with water so they would not catch fire, and they were so thick and heavy that the bales absorbed most of the cannon balls that struck them.

The shooting began on September 18, and continued almost without stop for 52 hours. It was an extremely bloody battle because the armies closed in to almost point-blank range. Finally, the Union army could bear no more losses and Colonel Mulligan surrendered. A cannonball from the battle is still lodged in the east column of the courthouse.

The **Anderson House**, now a museum, was used as a field hospital by both sides at various times as it changed hands during the battle. After the battle ended, General Price reported that his men had captured 3,000 prisoners, 5 pieces of artillery, 100 wagons, 300 muskets, about 1,000 horses, and recovered $900,000 of the money taken from the bank.

The **Battle of Lexington State Historic Park** is just outside of town. Trenches and earthworks from the battle have been preserved, and a mile-long interpretive trail tells the story.

About 11 miles south of Lexington on MO 13 near **Higginsville** is the **Confederate Memorial**, a 100-acre park with the **Old Confederate Soldiers' Home**, commemorating the 40,000 Missourians who died for the Confederate cause.

US 24 and MO 224 parallel each other along the Missouri River, with MO 224 finally disappearing at **Napoleon**. At **Buckner**, turn north on

Route BB to **Sibley**, where **Fort Osage** has been reconstructed. The first mention of the site is in the journals of Lewis and Clark on June 23, 1804. Here, in his engaging writing style with unpredictable spelling, is Clark's description of the area and of a small adventure that happened there:

> The wind was against us this morning . . . were obliged to lie-to during the day at a small island . . . directly opposite, on the south, is a high commanding position, more than 70 feet above the high water mark, and overlooking the river . . . . This spot has many advantages for a fort and trading house with the Indians.

They camped there that night and the next day Clark went ahead of the party to hunt. Clark continued:

> I Killed a Deer & made a fire, expecting the boat would come up in the evening, the wind continuing to blow prevented their moving, as the distance by land was too great for me to return by night I concluded to wood to make fired to keep off musquiturs & knats. Heard the party on Shore fire, at Dark Drewyer came to me with the horses, one fat bear & a Deer, river fell 8 Inches last night. . . .Set out at half after Six [the next day]. I joined the boat this morng at 8 oClock (I will only remark that dureing the time I lay on the sand waiting for the boat, a large Snake Swam to the bank imediately under the Deer which was hanging over the water, and no great distance from it, I threw chunks and drove this snake off Several times. I found that he was so determined on getting to the meet I was compelld to kill him, the part of the Deer which attracted this Snake I think was the Milk from the bag of the Doe.)

By 1808 Clark was territorial governor; he remembered the site and ordered Fort Osage to be built under his direction as the first United States outpost in the Louisiana Purchase. It was built both as a trading post with the Native Americans, and also to serve notice to the Spanish, British, as well as to the Native Americans that the United States meant business with the Louisiana Purchase. For the next five years, it was the westernmost outpost of the United States, until Fort Atkinson was built in 1813.

The fort was home to some of Missouri's pioneering families, including George Sibley, who made the fort a commercial success. Sibley courted

Fort Osage was built in 1808 soon after the Louisiana Purchase, and was the farthest western outpost of the U.S. for the next five years.

and won the hand of Mary Easton, the daughter of a wealthy banker in St. Louis, and when she joined her new husband it was with several keelboats filled with clothing and furniture. The Sibleys remained at the post until it was decommissioned, when they returned to St. Louis to found Lindenwood College, which is still in existence.

Fort Osage was eventually destroyed, and its ruins lay ignored for more than a century. In the early 1970s, the Friends of Fort Osage was created, which joined forces with the town of Sibley and the Jackson County Historical Society to rebuild the fort. It was declared a National Monument in the early 1980s and was given a federal grant. The restoration was completed in 1986 and the fort was taken over by **Jackson County Parks and Recreation**. It has a blacksmith shop and exhibits of trade goods. A living-history program offers conducted tours and special holiday candlelight programs.

From Sibley, you can return to US 24 the way you came or, if you have a detailed local map with you, you can follow a series of smaller roads across the bottomland into Independence or Kansas City. You might also consider driving north of Lexington to the small town of Richmond, which immodestly proclaims itself the mushroom capital of the world. For the purposes of this book, you may want to see the statue of the Mexican War hero, Alexander Doniphan, rather than mushrooms growing in the dark.

IN THE AREA

Arrow Rock has a few bed-and-breakfasts and places to eat. Since most business is conducted from June until early October, visitor amenities remain modest. Most B&Bs are open year-round. Two have five guest rooms and two others have two guest rooms.

Arrow Rock B&B, Arrow Rock. Call 800-795-2797. On the National Historic Register and the only B&B that offers dinner as well as the expected breakfast. In this case, the breakfast includes raspberries grown in the garden.

Arrow Rock Station Bed and Breakfast, 502 W. Main Street, Arrow Rock. Call 660-837-3210. Serves lunch and dinner and has two bedrooms for B&B customers. The building was intended as a service station when it was built in 1931. It then became a convenience store that sold gasoline, and finally in 1976 it became a restaurant. Everything is cooked on-site using non-frozen meats and mostly in-season vegetables, plus rolls and desserts. It seats up to 75 customers and serves American cuisine.

Historic Arrow Rock Tavern, Arrow Rock. Call 660-837-3200. Dating back to 1834, this tavern is open March through December and serves lunch and dinner. It also offers banquets.

OTHER CONTACTS

Arrow Rock State Historic Site and Park. Call 660-837-3330. Web site: www.mostateparks.com/arrowrock/camp.htm.

Historic Arrow Rock Council. Call 660-837-3470.

Lexington Chamber of Commerce. Call 816-259-2040. Web site: www.historiclexington.com.

Battle of Lexington State Historic Site. Call 816-259-4654. Web site: www.mostateparks.com/lexington/.

Fort Osage County Park. Call 816-881-4431.

Acknowledgments

As usual, I am indebted to several people for their generosity and encouragement while I was working on this book. I received excellent support from the Missouri Division of Tourism, especially from Tracey Berry of the tourism staff, and Holly Milledge and Jessica Taveau who worked for public relations firms dealing with the Division of Tourism.

In something of a catchall statement, I want to thank the many Missourians whose names I didn't get but who went out of their way to be kind to me, for no other reason than I was a stranger and needed information. This includes the cabdriver in Grain Valley who, without my asking, explained that he didn't use a meter but charged by the mile and showed me the mileages he wrote on his pad. The desk clerk of the Shilo Inn at Independence who allowed me to leave my luggage in the lobby while waiting for the airport shuttle, insisted I have a cup of coffee, and refused a tip when I left. I am also grateful to the woman and teenage girls who were running a book sale outside the public library in Kirksville. They charged me 25 cents for eight issues of the *Missouri Historical Review* and were disappointed that I didn't take the whole box at the same price.

Lest you think I have been so overcome with nostalgia that I can see no wrong in Missouri, I found that there are always exceptions; two incidents I'll mention were so out of character I thought they were funny. One occurred in a small hotel in Hannibal. I walked in and the clerk looked up from the chair he was repairing and snapped, "Just what is it you want?" I had wanted a room, but decided I wanted out. The same thing occurred when a chain motel on I-70 tried to charge me $15 over the quoted rate for a nonsmoking room. There is only one Eden.

Some wise and honest writer once said that he stood on the shoulders of giants, meaning that his book was only as good as the other books, articles, and sundry materials he read while researching his book. Before writing this book, I read several books and bought several, so I could take a bit of Missouri home with me.

As with so many books about a place, the author is indebted to several people for helping in a variety of ways. Friends dating back to high school offered good advice, and in some cases did actual research. Rex Hickox not only sent several emails and a package of brochures, he enlisted his brother Gary to dig up some information. Marilee Easley Barnard also offered suggestions, and made phone calls for the author. Bob Anderson of the U.S. Army Corps of Engineers answered a series of questions the best way possible for a writer: He sent a CD that was loaded with articles, a book-length manuscript on New Madrid, and dozens of historical photographs, all available for my use.

Following are some of the more useful books and articles I found, especially the first two listed. The WPA Guide series is still, after 60 years, the best collection of guides ever written in the United States. I relied heavily on this volume for historical and cultural history. Bill Earngey's book is equally helpful and I urge readers to buy a copy.

After buying several state maps, and wearing out my welcome at the local AAA office, I finally bought a set of maps that are more durable than any others. The *Missouri Atlas & Gazetteer* (DeLorme) has everything I needed, including immunity to spilled coffee.

Bibliography

Bittersweet, Inc. *Bittersweet Country*. Edited by Ellen Gray Massey. Garden City, NY: Anchor Press, 1978.

Capper/Midwest Research Institute. *The Missouri Quick-Fact Book*. Topeka, KS: The Capper Press, 1991.

Dawson, Joseph C. III. *Doniphan's Epic March: The 1st Missouri Volunteers in the Mexican War*. Lawrence, KS: University Press of Kansas,1999.

Earngey, Bill. *Missouri Roadsides: The Traveler's Companion*. Columbia, MO: The University of Missouri Press, 1995.

Hagwood, J. Hurley, and Roberta Hurley. "Peg-Leg Shannon." Unpublished manuscript. Missouri Historical Society Library.

Howard, Guy. *Walkin' Preacher of the Ozarks*. New York: Harper & Brothers, 1944.

Hubbell, Sue. "Earthquake Fever." *The New Yorker*, February 11, 1991.

In the Heart of Ozark Mountain Country. Edited by Frank Reuter. Reeds Spring, MO: White Oak Publishing, 1993.

——— . *Borderland Rebellion*. Branson, MO: The Ozarks Mountaineer, 1980.

Ingenthron, Elmo. *Indians of the Ozark Plateau*. Branson, MO: The Ozarks Mountaineer, 1970, renewed 1983.

Kurz, Don. *Scenic Driving the Ozarks*. Helena, MT: Falcon Publishing, 1996.

Nagel, Paul C. *Missouri: A History.* Lawrence, KS: University Press of Kansas, 1977.

New Madrid Historical Museum. *Some Happenings of the New Madrid Earthquake 1811–1812.* Compiled by Dorothy H. Halstead.

Roads & Their Builders. Missouri State Highway Commission's Division of Public Information.

Works Progress Administration. *The WPA Guide to 1930s Missouri.* Lawrence, KS: University Press of Kansas, 1986.

Yater, George H., and Carolyn S. Dentgon. *Nine Young Men from Kentucky: We Proceeded On.* The Lewis and Clark Trail Heritage Foundation, Inc., 1992.

Index